THE BALANCE OF PAYMENTS:
FREE VERSUS FIXED
EXCHANGE RATES

*Fourth in the series of Rational Debate Seminars
sponsored by the American Enterprise Institute
held at
The George Washington University
Washington, D. C.*

THE
BALANCE OF PAYMENTS:
FREE VERSUS FIXED
EXCHANGE RATES

Milton Friedman
Robert V. Roosa

RATIONAL DEBATE SEMINARS

American Enterprise Institute
for Public Policy Research
Washington, D. C.

Second Printing, June 1973

Library of Congress Catalog Card Number 672307

FOREWORD

Rational debate, with the emphasis on "rational," is the keystone of a free society. This is the concept on which the American Enterprise Institute was founded in 1943 and on which it continues to operate today. This book records the fourth in a new series of Rational Debates sponsored by the Institute to explore major public issues. The format was devised to avoid what happens too often in the course of debating vital public issues, a degeneration into repetitious absolutes which do not present rational choices. The choice, of course, is seldom between the wholly good or the wholly bad. Far from being simple, most public issues evoke a wide spectrum of arguments requiring careful consideration. We are confident that Dr. Roosa and Professor Friedman have illuminated the grays as well as the blacks and whites in the issue of free versus fixed exchange rates.

The purpose of AEI from its inception has been to help legislators, policymakers, educators, the press, and the general public to reach informed judgments on major issues of public policy. The Institute conducts research, publishes studies, and sponsors seminars and symposia on major questions of the day. Statements by lecturers and other participants in AEI projects are their own. The Institute itself takes no position on any public policy issue.

In the 1966-67 academic year, the American Enterprise Institute presented four Rational Debates on major public policy issues. The first, *Congress and the Presidency: Their Role in Modern Times,* featured Arthur Schlesinger, Jr., and Alfred de Grazia. The second pitted Charles E. Whittaker against William Sloane Coffin, Jr., on *Law, Order and Civil Disobedience.* The third Rational Debate, on "The New Economics," brought together Arthur F. Burns and Paul A. Samuelson. This is the fourth and final debate of the 1966-67 series.

It is the hope of the American Enterprise Institute that these seminars will contribute to wise policy decisions at all levels of the governments of the United States, federal, state, and local.

July 10, 1967   William J. Baroody
                       President
                       American Enterprise Institute
                          for Public Policy Research

PREFACE

Dr. Roosa and Professor Friedman have given us, in this fourth of the Rational Debate Series, an unusual opportunity to compare two well-reasoned, brilliantly argued views of the United States' balance-of-payments problems. In their frank exchanges there is less of the gloss and more of the fundamentals than one finds in most lengthier discourses on this difficult subject.

The Friedman-Roosa debate's three sessions, spanning two weeks last May, were attended by a small, select group of government officials, academicians, and newsmen. Now the public at large can study the speakers' lectures and rebuttals, as well as their responses to questions from the other participants.

This event brought to a close the first academic season of Rational Debates sponsored by the American Enterprise Institute, whose diligence in informing public opinion on the pros and cons of major policy issues has helped to reinvigorate the nation's intellect in a time of expanding need.

July 9, 1967

G. Warren Nutter
Coordinator
Rational Debate Series

CONTENTS

FIRST LECTURE

MILTON FRIEDMAN

Economists may not know much. But we do know one thing very well: how to produce shortages and surpluses. Do you want to produce a shortage of any product? Simply have government fix and enforce a legal *maximum* price on the product which is less than the price that would otherwise prevail. That is how the great housing "shortage" of postwar years was produced—by legal fixing of maximum rents. That is why New York City which is the only city in the country that still has legal rent control is also the only city that still has a housing shortage of the wartime type.

Do you want to produce a surplus of any product? Simply have government fix and enforce a legal *minimum* price above the price that would otherwise prevail, either by making it illegal to pay less or by offering to buy all that is offered at that price. That is why there is a surplus of unskilled youths seeking jobs—because the government makes it illegal for enterprises to pay less than the legal minimum wage. That is why we were plagued for so many years by agricultural surpluses—because the government pegged farm prices at levels above those that would have cleared the market.

The same fixed price may at one time produce a surplus and at another a shortage. An excellent example is the price of silver. When, at the end of 1933, the U.S. government first offered to buy all newly produced domestic silver at 64-64/99 cents an ounce, this price was well above the price that would clear the market—at the end of 1932, silver had been selling on the open market for as low as 25 cents an ounce. The result of this action plus the subsequent Silver Purchase Act of 1934 which authorized purchases abroad as well, plus subsequent rises in the fixed price, was a veritable flood of silver. We drained China, Mexico, and the rest of the world, more than tripling our stocks of silver. Since 1955, however, the price has been below the price that would clear the market—thanks to price inflation at home and abroad and despite further rises in the pegged price to $1.29. As a result, there is now a shortage instead of a surplus. We are keeping the price down only by rapidly depleting our reserves. We shall be forced to let it rise sometime in the next few years.*

Wheat may be or may become another example. For many years, the great problem was the surplus generated by our pegged price. We were forced to build mammoth storage facilities, to impose extensive restrictions and controls on farmers to keep down their output, to tolerate a different price at home and abroad, controlling foreign trade in wheat in order to do so. Now, as world

---

* As occurred not long after the lecture was delivered.

population and food needs are booming and inflation proceeds on its merry way, the pegged wheat price may be or may become too low. If so, our stocks will be rapidly drained.

As these examples suggest, the technique of fixing prices is an extremely powerful tool. The result will often appear far out of proportion to the cause. Fix the price only a little too high and there will appear to be a tremendous surplus because the price will simultaneously discourage buyers and encourage sellers. In addition, it will cause the disappointed sellers to make multiple offers which will make the supply look larger than it is. Every attempt to curtail supply by government regulation will be met by the ingenuity of the myriad of private suppliers trying to find some way around the regulations, so that there will be a continual tug-of-war, with the regulations piling ever higher. Fix the price only a little too low and there will appear to be a tremendous shortage, because the price will simultaneously encourage buyers and discourage sellers. In addition, disappointed buyers will stand, or have stand-ins, in more than one queue.

The situation is reminiscent of Micawber's law, as reported by Charles Dickens, "Annual income twenty pounds, annual expenditure nineteen six, result happiness. Annual income twenty pounds, annual expenditure twenty pounds ought and six, result misery."

The apparent disproportion between cause and effect is the major hindrance—as I have discovered again and again—to public understanding of the phenomenon. How can it be, the ordinary man is likely to say, that prohibiting landlords from raising the rent—surely no more than a simple act of justice—can have such far-reaching effects as long lists of people seeking apartments relative to apartments available, widespread complaints of a shortage of housing space—even though the number of dwelling units per person may be at its all-time maximum—the development of black markets, the deterioration of rental housing, and so on and on? Can it be, the same intelligent layman is likely to say, that the entire complicated farm surplus problem, with its panoply of regulations, elections among farmers, plowing under of hogs, taking land out of cultivation—that this whole problem simply reflects government's attempt to assure parity prices for farmers? Surely something more basic and fundamental must be involved.

Yet the truth is, nothing more is involved. Fix prices—and the problems will multiply; let prices find their own level in free markets—and the problems will disappear. The abolition of rent control everywhere in the United States except New York City shortly after the war is one dramatic example. The "shortages" disappeared almost overnight. The real problems of high cost of building and of urban blight of course remained—but the false problems disappeared. And in this case, New York City remained as a control to illuminate the source of the problems. The abolition of price control in Germany by Ludwig Erhard one Sunday afternoon in 1948 is another and even more dramatic example. That was all it took to release Germany from the chains that were producing stagnation at a level of output half the prewar level and to permit the German miracle to occur.

All of this may seem far afield from my announced topic but it is not. The problem of the balance of payments is simply another example of the far-reaching effects of government price fixing, complicated only by two facts: first, that two sets of prices are involved—the price of gold in terms of various national currencies, and the price of national currencies in terms of one another; second, that more than one country is involved.

The existence of two sets of prices is a relic of an earlier day, when there was a real gold standard, and "dollar," "pound," and "franc" were simply names for different amounts of gold. Under such a gold standard, government's role is primarily simply as a mint, to certify the weight and fineness of the gold, coin it on demand, issue warehouse certificates for gold, and redeem the certificates—though in practice governments also issued promises to pay gold not fully backed by gold. Under such a system, exchange rates were kept in narrow bounds—within the "gold points"—not by government price fixing but by the private shipment of gold whenever the market price varied by enough to make it worthwhile to acquire a foreign currency by shipping gold rather than by an exchange transaction. Exchange rates stayed within narrow limits for the same reason and in the same way that the price of sugar in New York

never deviates much from the price of sugar in Chicago
—because if it did deviate, it would pay private traders
to ship sugar.

The movements of gold that kept exchange rates in
line also served to produce adjustments that made the
gold flows self-limiting. The country shipping gold experienced a decline in the quantity of money; the country receiving gold, a rise. The monetary changes in turn
affected incomes and prices, and therewith the demand
for foreign exchange, lowering the demand in the country shipping gold, and raising it in the country receiving
gold. The key feature of this process was that it was
completely automatic and gradual. There was no way the
gold movements could be prevented from affecting the
money stock. A small discrepancy called forth a small
adjustment. There was a unified currency system, not a
collection of national currencies linked by fixed rates.
Such a unified currency exists today among the different
states of the U.S., between Britain and some of its co-
lonial territories, like Hong Kong, and in many similar
cases, but not among such areas.

The situation today is clearly very different. Gold is a
commodity whose price is supported by the government
—like wheat or butter. The major difference is that we
support the price only for foreigners not for U.S. citizens, since it is illegal for U.S. citizens to hold gold except
for numismatic or industrial purposes. In addition, gold
has the special property that at the moment there is a
highly elastic foreign demand for it, so we can always sell

it to acquire foreign exchange. Clearly, we could peg the price of gold even though exchange rates were not fixed. For example, Canada's having a floating exchange rate, as it did from 1950 to 1962, did not prevent us from continuing to peg the price of gold even though Canada is a large producer of gold. There would have been a conflict only if Canada had also tried to peg the price in terms of Canadian currency.

The levels at which exchange rates are now fixed are calculated from the official price of gold each nation lists with the International Monetary Fund. But it is clear that exchange rates are not kept within narrow bounds by the movement of gold. Most countries that have fixed exchange rates with one another do not freely buy and sell gold. The U.S. does indirectly on the London gold market with the cooperation of the Bank of England, but it does so in order to peg the gold price, just as we sell silver to peg the silver price, not as the primary means of fixing exchange rates. We could abandon the pegging of the price of gold and yet continue to peg exchange rates, just as the pegging of exchange rates does not require the pegging of the price of lead, or copper, or steel. Gold is now at most window dressing, not the king pin of the monetary system that determines the quantity of money. Hence, I propose in this paper to concentrate on exchange rates, leaving mostly to one side, as a subsidiary issue, the price of gold.

The second complication is that more than one government is involved. Consider, for specificity, the case of Britain and the United States. The official price of the pound sterling in terms of the dollar is $2.80, but our agreement with the IMF permits the price to fluctuate a bit on each side of that, roughly between $2.82 and $2.78. The U.S. is committed to keeping the price from rising above $2.82—since that would constitute a depreciation of the U.S. currency; the British are committed to keeping the price from falling below $2.78— since that would constitute a depreciation of the British currency. Of course, there is nothing to prevent either country from engaging in transactions that help the other keep its commitment, but that is the formal division of responsibility.

The U.S. can keep the price from rising above $2.82 only by offering to sell all the pounds demanded at that price—i.e., to buy all the dollars offered; the British can keep the price from falling below $2.78 only by offering to buy all the pounds offered at that price—i.e., to sell all the dollars demanded at that price. How can the two countries succeed?

Suppose, that, at a price of $2.82 per pound, the number of dollars that people or governments wish to use to buy pounds in order to spend, lend, or give away is greater than the number of dollars that other people or governments wish to acquire with pounds. Suppose, that is, that the U.S. has a potential balance-of-payments deficit. How can the U.S. keep the price at $2.82? Clearly, there are basically only two ways: by providing the additional pounds, either out of its own reserves of foreign exchange or by borrowing them from someone else; or by inducing or forcing people to change the number of pounds they seek to buy. And the converse statements hold for the British in the contrary case.

To use the language that has become common, there are two problems: the liquidity problem—having enough reserves to be able to meet demands; the adjustment problem—keeping demand in line with supply. This is the precise counterpart of the problem for wheat: the liquidity problem—accumulating or decumulating wheat stocks; the adjustment problem—keeping down the production of wheat or stimulating its consumption.

Superficially, it looks as if the liquidity problem could be easily solved simply by reversing the tasks assigned the United States and Britain. Let Britain keep the price of the pound sterling from rising above $2.82 by offering to sell an unlimited number of pounds at that price and let the United States keep the price of the pound from falling below $2.78 by offering to buy an unlimited number of pounds at that price. Each can always do so. Britain manufactures pounds and the United States manufactures dollars, so each can always meet its commitments. However, in doing so, each is in effect giving the other country a blank check on its own goods and serices. If the price of the pound were tending to rise, Britain would be accumulating dollars. The counterpart would be a flow of goods from Britain to the United States. Britain would in effect be giving the United States an unintended loan at a zero interest rate. This is precisely what happened to Germany for many years: it accepted a large inflow of dollars, which meant that it was selling a larger dollar volume of goods than it was buying; it was implicitly exporting goods on credit. Clearly no country will be willing to do this indefinitely.

Yet this approach is worth mentioning, because it is the lure that underlies all the talk of an international agreement to create "paper gold," new international reserves. At bottom, what is involved is an agreement by countries to make automatic loans to one another. Every country will be in favor of such an agreement, in principle. But each will want a different agreement—one that enables it to borrow much and commits it to lending little. Thus I predict, without fear of successful contradiction, that despite all the appearance of agreement in principle, no effective agreement will in fact be reached.

To return to the United States' liquidity problem. The alternative to Britain's providing an unlimited line of credit at zero interest is for the United States to build up reserves in advance from which it can meet excess demands for pounds—this is indeed the important role played by our gold stocks—or to arrange to borrow as the occasion demands.

Clearly, potential deficits cannot be met indefinitely out of reserves. Reserves are necessarily limited. Clearly, also, to meet the deficits indefinitely by governmental borrowing abroad would be costly and undesirable. And, on the other side, no country will be willing to accumulate another country's currency indefinitely. *Reserves alone cannot do the job*. There must be some adjustment mechanism.

What possible adjustment mechanisms are there? One is the standard gold-standard mechanism—changes in the quantity of money, income, and prices internally. After all, the only reason a problem arises is because the existence of central banks interferes with this mechanism. With central banks, a payment deficit need not mean a reduction in the quantity of money, because the central bank can offset it, and a surplus need not mean an increase. Indeed, central banks are a necessary—and today almost a sufficient—condition for a balance-of-payments problem.

A central bank could do deliberately what the real gold standard did automatically. To correct the United States balance-of-payments deficit, it could reduce the quantity of money (or reduce the rate of growth), lowering incomes and prices—or letting them rise less rapidly than in other countries. This would reduce the demand for foreign exchange and increase its supply.

The United States has done this to some extent. It is clear-that monetary policy was tighter than it otherwise would have been from 1956-61 because of the balance-of-payments problem. But it is also clear that it is both unlikely that the United States would put major reliance on this adjustment mechanism and undesirable that it should do so. It is unlikely because of the government's commitment to full employment. It is almost inconceivable that any administration, of either party, would be willing to force a significant domestic recession or depression to resolve a balance-of-payments problem. It is undesirable that the United States put major reliance on this adjustment mechanism partly because foreign trade is so small a part of our economy—it is absurd to force 95 percent of the economy to adjust to 5 percent rather than the other way around. More basically, it is undesirable because many of the adjustments forced on us are likely to be the product not of changes in the real forces of demand or supply but of monetary manipulations of other countries.

This adjustment mechanism is the one which the proponents of fixed rates regard as the "discipline" imposed by the fixed-rate system. But it is a peculiar discipline. The discipline of fixed rates forced inflation on Germany in the past decade at least as effectively as it forced deflation on us. The only discipline is to keep in step with the rest of the world, not to march in the right direction. In any event, it is clearly a discipline that we are not willing to accept.

The only other adjustment mechanism—while pegging exchange rates—is to control by direct or indirect means the amount of foreign exchange people try to buy—the counterpart to restrictions on the production of wheat. Britain and other countries have, of course, extensive exchange control. A resident of Britain may not exchange pounds for dollars without the explicit permission of a government official. This has involved extraordinarily detailed control of the day-to-day life of the British citizen—where he may go on a vacation, what books he may read, and so on, ad infinitum.

We have so far avoided explicit exchange control, but we have interfered in many ways with private trade —some serious, some niggling, some demeaning. Oil import quotas, meat quotas, and quotas and tariffs on many other products have been justified as means of "saving" foreign exchange. The niggling reduction of the duty-free tourist's allowance has the same origin. So has the demeaning spectacle of our negotiating "voluntary" quotas on exports from Hong Kong and Singapore and Japan. Our high officials have gone hat-in-hand to France and Germany and other countries to plead for earlier repayments of loans and special purchases of American goods. We have required recipients of foreign aid to buy American goods—giving with one hand and taking away with the other. We have preached free trade and practiced restriction. And most recently, we have gone in for "voluntary" controls on foreign lending by banks and foreign investment by enterprises. And the end is not yet.

With all this we have not succeeded. The experience of countless price-fixing schemes has been repeated. Let the fixed price differ from the price that would clear the market, and it will take herculean efforts to hold it.

Consequently, we have also been driven to the final adjustment mechanism—changes in the exchange rate. We profess to have kept the exchange rate rigid. Yet we have in effect devalued it selectively. That is what the interest equalization tax amounts to. For purposes of buying foreign securities, the dollar has been devalued by 15 percent, and a further devaluation is proposed. That is also what our program of reducing the foreign exchange component of military expenditures amounts to. Our military authorities are instructed to compare the cost in dollars at the official exchange rate of purchasing an item abroad with the cost in dollars of buying it in the United States. If the cost in the United States exceeds the foreign cost by less than x percent, they are instructed to buy it at home—paradoxically to save dollars. I do not know what x is but I understand that it is sizable, something over 50 percent. The tying of foreign aid is another example.

We sneer at South American countries that adopt multiple exchange rate systems. Yet that is what we have adopted—only in concealed form.

There is one and only one satisfactory solution: abolish governmental price fixing. Let exchange rates become free market prices determined primarily by private dealings. Let the government simply stay out of the picture.

Suppose, under such a system, that, at a price of $2.80 to the pound, the number of dollars that people want to use to buy pounds to spend, lend, or give away is greater than the number of dollars holders of pounds want to acquire. The eager buyers will offer to pay more. The price of the pound will be bid up. As it rises, buyers of pounds will be discouraged—because a higher price of the pound means a higher price in dollars for goods and services bought abroad—and the sellers of pounds will be encouraged—because a higher price of the pound means that they can buy more United States goods and services with a given number of pounds. At some price, say $3.08, the number of dollars offered will be equal to the number of dollars demanded.

This rise in the price of the pound by 10 percent will have had precisely the same effect on the relative costs to Americans and Britons of American and British goods as a decline of 10 percent in United States prices with no change in British prices, or a rise of 10 percent in British prices with no change in United States prices. But how much easier it is to have the exchange rate change by 10 percent than to get a *general* decline in all United States prices by 10 percent. Why not have one price—and that a potentially highly flexible one—do the adjusting rather than require the myriads of domestic prices to vary, with all their stickiness and all the side effects? Why not have the dog wag the tail, instead of the tail wag the dog?

As this example suggests, a system of floating exchange rates completely eliminates the balance-of-payments problem—just as in a free market there cannot be a surplus or a shortage in the sense of eager sellers unable to find buyers or eager buyers unable to find sellers. The price may fluctuate but there cannot be a deficit or a surplus threatening an exchange crisis. Floating exchange rates would put an end to the grave problems requiring repeated meetings of secretaries of the Treasury and governors of central banks to try to draw up sweeping reforms. It would put an end to the occasional crisis producing frantic scurrying of high governmental officials from capital to capital, midnight phone calls among the great central banks lining up emergency loans to support one or another currency.

Indeed this is, I believe, one of the major sources of the opposition to floating exchange rates. The people engaged in these activities are important people and they are all persuaded that they are engaged in important activities. It cannot be, they say to themselves, that these important activities arise simply from pegging exchange rates. They must have more basic roots. Hence, they say, it is simpleminded to believe that freeing exchange rates would eliminate the problem. That is what the allied advisers engaged in price control, rationing, and the like told Erhard that summer in 1948. That is why he removed price controls on a Sunday, when they were not in their offices to countermand his edicts.

Under a system of floating exchange rates, the liquidity problem disappears. There is no need for official foreign exchange reserves. Private individuals will provide the reserves needed—just as they do in commodities that trade in a free market. If a given movement in exchange rates seems temporary, it will be in the self-interest of private holders of exchange to dampen the move by speculation and they can be counted on to do so.

With floating rates, we could therefore terminate at once the frustrating and ineffective negotiations for a new international liquidity arrangement—negotiations that are in any event bound to fail. More important, we could abolish at once the interest-equalization tax and informal exchange controls.

Most important of all, floating rates would enable us to separate issues and determine our national policies on the right grounds. Monetary and fiscal policy could be directed toward pursuing internal stability without being hamstrung by the balance of payments. We could decide how much foreign aid to give in terms of our resources and our values, not by the irrelevant consideration of the currency in which it is expressed. We could instruct the military to buy in the cheapest market and keep the real costs to a minimum—not turn them into a foreign exchange authority. We could conduct foreign policy in terms of our true national interests—not in terms of the effect on gold flows. We could behave in foreign trade like a great nation, not like a mendicant, by unilaterally moving toward freer trade without having to be concerned about balance-of-payments problems.

This last point perhaps deserves a slight digression. Not the least of the advantages of floating rates, in my opinion, is that it makes it so much easier for the layman to understand the merits of free trade. With rigid rates, the first effect of a reduction in tariffs is an increase in imports without any immediate effect on exports. It looks as if imports have simply displaced domestic products and so produced unemployment. It takes a subtle chain of reasoning to show that this is only part of the story, that the increase in imports will have indirect effects that will ultimately lead to an expansion of exports so that the final result is an increase in foreign trade not an increase in unemployment. And, indeed, with our present nearly paralyzed adjustment mechanism, the indirect effects may be long delayed and highly unreliable.

With floating rates, a reduction in tariffs will also produce an attempted increase in imports. But how can this be realized? Only if the importers can get some foreign exchange. To do so they will bid up its price which immediately makes exports more attractive to foreigners. The first effect of a reduction in tariffs is thus a rise in the price of foreign exchange and a simultaneous increase in imports and exports. There is not even a temporary importation of unemployment.

The floating rate provides the protection to the balance of payments that is essential if we are to move significantly to ease barriers to trade. In the absence of such protection, it appears as if we can afford to reduce barriers only in return for a reciprocal reduction of barriers by others. The result is the kind of drawn-out and ineffective negotiations that are currently nearing their appointed end in connection with the Kennedy round.

What objections have been raised against floating rates?

One is the allegation that we cannot move to floating rates on our own, that just as two governments are now involved in pegging each rate, so it will take two to unpeg. This is in one sense correct, yet it is irrelevant. The United States can announce that it will no longer try to keep the dollar from depreciating—i.e., in the case of the pound, no longer try to prevent the price of the pound from rising above $2.82. If Britain wants to take on the task of keeping the price of the pound from rising, fine. It can do so only by either being willing to accumulate dollars indefinitely—which is to say, by extending us an unlimited line of credit—or by adapting its internal policy to ours, so that the free market rate stays below $2.82. In either case, we can only gain not lose. Similarly, if it chooses to continue to keep the price of the pound from falling, that again is no cause for concern on our part. It can only do so by using dollar reserves, which we must be ready to permit, or again by aligning its internal policy with ours.

I think it highly likely that if we announced that our government will no longer intervene in the exchange market, a fair number of other countries would peg their currencies to ours. I see no harm in that and much good. Perhaps we could begin to build up a truly unified currency area—not a collection of national currencies linked by pegged rates. A system of floating exchange rates has basically much more in common with a real gold standard—in that both leave private individuals free to buy and sell currencies as they wish and both are free of government intervention—than either has with our present system.

A second objection that is raised is that floating exchange rates would be highly unstable and that unstable rates would add to the uncertainty and difficulty of conducting foreign trade. However, floating rates need not be highly unstable. Canada had floating rates from 1950 to 1962 and they were highly stable. If floating rates are highly unstable, it will be because the internal monetary policies of the countries or some other aspects of their economy are highly unstable. But in that case, the uncertainty is there and the only question is what form it takes. Under a real gold standard, the uncertainty would be about internal price levels, because they would reflect the instability. Under pegged exchange rates, the uncertainty would be about whether exchange would be available, that is, what the exchange controls would be like. If anything, the uncertainty about the price of foreign exchange under a floating rate system is the easiest for a trader to protect himself against by hedging in a futures market.

A related argument is that the uncertainty under floating rates would be greater than under other systems because floating rates would give rise to destabilizing speculation. When I first began writing on this subject nearly two decades ago, I took this objection seriously. I no longer do. In the interim, there have been a considerable number of careful empirical studies of speculation under floating rates. None has produced a clear example of destabilizing speculation on any significant scale. And the bulk of the evidence strongly supports the view that speculation has generally been clearly stabilizing. I think it is time therefore that this bug-a-boo is given a decent burial —at least until somebody can come up with some real evidence that it is more than a bug-a-boo.

Another objection to floating rates is that it reduces the attractiveness of a country as a financial center. This can be correct. It may well be that Britain was at one time well advised on this score to maintain rigid rates with other countries or that Switzerland is now. But this seems to me not a relevant objection for the United States. First, our international financial activity is not a major industry. Second, its development is interfered with at least as much by the measures—like the interest equalization tax and "voluntary" controls on foreign lending—that we take to peg the rates as it would be by floating rates. Third, the formation of a "dollar" bloc, suggested as a possibility above, might be a favorable development. Fourth, without the interest equalization tax, informal exchange controls, and extensive trade barriers, the dollar would very likely be used even more extensively than it is as an international currency. Paradoxical though it seems, letting rates float, and removing controls, may be the most effective way to strengthen New York's role as a financial center.

The major objection raised against floating rates is one already mentioned—that it would remove the "discipline" which fixed rates are said to impose on domestic economic policy, that it would open the door to irresponsible inflationary monetary policy. This objection has merit if the alternative were a real gold standard. It has some merit for countries like Italy and Japan that have been susceptible to highly inflationary policies, that have been willing to submit to the discipline of the balance of payments, and for which foreign trade is a substantial part of total trade. It has negligible merit for the United States. Foreign trade is so small a part of total trade, and our reserves are so large, that we can neglect the balance of payments for long stretches of time, letting small disturbances build up into big ones. And even then, we are not willing to submit to the discipline. Instead, we resort to import quotas, tariffs, multiple exchange rates, and informal exchange controls. The same discipline which produced these, incidentally also produced inflationary pressure from 1945 to 1956 when we were accumulating gold and foreign exchange. The discipline is asymmetrical: we yield to it when it imposes inflation on us; we resist it when it calls for deflation. That is a kind of discipline that I think we can do without.

These are the objections to floating rates. But they are not the reasons why we do not—and very likely shall not —adopt floating rates.

The most important reason we stick to pegged rates is the tyranny of the status quo. The United States has taken the public position that the dollar will be defended. The President and other high officials have committed themselves over and over again to the proposition that the dollar will not be devalued, that the present system of pegged rates is one of the great postwar achievements, which the United States will support with might and main. Once such a position is taken, it takes a major crisis to produce a change.

A second reason is the confusion between a real gold standard and the pseudo-gold standard we now have. The public at large and in particular the financial community hankers after the freedom from government intervention of a real gold standard. It confuses the pegged rates of our present system with the rigid rates of a real gold standard.

A third reason is the confusion between devaluation and a system of floating rates. A particular exchange problem can be met by changing the level at which the exchange rate is pegged. Such a system, under which the level at which the exchange rate is pegged is changed at substantial intervals of time, is the worst of both worlds. An adjustable peg provides neither the certainty of a truly fixed rate nor the flexibility of a floating rate. It is certain to be subject to destabilizing speculation. Such a system must be sharply distinguished from a system of floating rates. Devaluation of the dollar to a new pegged level would, in my opinion, be most unwise; whereas establishment of a system of floating rates is eminently to be desired.

A final reason is what may be called the Arizona effect. As you may know, the death rate from tuberculosis is higher in Arizona than in any other state in the country. Clearly, Arizona must be a most unhealthy place to live.

Similarly, floating exchange rates have often been adopted as a last resort by countries experiencing grave financial crises when all other devices have failed. That is a major reason why they have such a bad reputation.

SECOND LECTURE

ROBERT V. ROOSA

Any debate on a subject as vast as the balance of payments needs narrowing down to particular issues. Fortunately this one, as I understand the intention of our sponsors, is to be centered on the special significance of the exchange rate in balance-of-payments adjustment. That relieves me of any need for introductory remarks on the current plight of the United States, and projects me right into a few generalizations about the relations between external and internal adjustments in a modern economy. After that brief preface, I can take up my main theme—that the best way to understand the value of the present system of fixed exchange rates is to see what would be wrong with a system of "free" or "flexible" rates.

A country's external accounts, summarized through the flows recorded in its balance of payments, are understandably important for what they show, looking outward, about the country's economic relations with the rest of the world. These accounts may, when in deficit, or in surplus, or even at times when in equilibrium, point to distortions that need correction in the country's own behavior toward foreign trade or aid or capital movements. Or they may simply show that disturbances or deficiencies elsewhere are creating difficulties for a particular country. But a country's balance-of-payments accounts can also be important for what they frequently reveal, looking inward, about the country's own domestic economy—whether it is achieving the mix of saving, investment, and consumption, or of prices and wages and profits, or of commodities, industries, and services, for example, that would be most likely to assure sustained advances in employment, incomes, and general welfare at home.

Not only outwardly but also inwardly, then, the balance of payments can have a pervasive significance for the economic policy of any nation. Over and above all this, for us, of course, there are the special balance-of-payments concerns of the United States as the supplier of much of the world's internationally usable money, and the special implications of this country's dominant size as both exporter and importer, and lender and borrower—serving in effect as a pivot for the movements of money, trade, and capital throughout the world. But what I want to stress, from the very outset, is my own conviction that the balance of payments of this country or of any country often mirrors, in outline if not in detail, the mistakes and the achievements of its own domestic economy.

In general, a country whose external accounts are seriously and continually out of balance often has something going seriously awry within its own economy, and a look through the window provided by the balance-of-payments accounts will usually help to locate the cause. This proposition is not particularly novel when it is expressed concerning countries in deficit. But countries with sustained large surpluses, though less likely to be urgently concerned, will also usually find that their swollen earnings are partly the result of conditions at home that will need correction or adjustment sooner or later in order to avoid potential (or possibly even present) difficulties in the domestic economy.

To many of my economist friends the comments I have just made are not merely polite introductory clichés, but challenging, fighting words. For I am really saying that balance-of-payments viability is, or should be, among the principal tests and guides for the functioning of domestic economic policy. And in the context of the topic for tonight's discussion, I am going to go further and assert that this essential, indeed inescapable, testing, guiding, or even "disciplining" that the outside world provides for each individual national economy is what, in the end, impels all countries toward some sort of approximation of a market economy. It seems to me that national economies simply project on a wider canvas, and in their own more complicated way, images of many of the same problems and the same needs that we identify much more familiarly with individual firms, and the relations among firms. I even suspect, or at any rate can hope, that Professor Friedman will agree that movement toward the characteristic relationships of the market economy is as relevant for the flourishing of nations as for firms.

I must concede, of course, that the path toward the market economy is very long and roundabout for many countries—measured in generations rather than in years. I must also concede that the working out of balance-of-payments disciplines often occurs in strange ways— harsh, crude, and extreme. But what I want to argue, while enjoying the privilege of joining issues with one of the world's most distinguished exponents of market economics, is that a system of fixed rates of currency exchange provides the most hospitable environment for encouraging market-oriented adjustments within and among nations.

To do that I will first have to state a little more concisely what it is that I mean by a fixed exchange rate system, and contrast that with several variants of flexible exchange rates. After identifying my side of this argument, I can return for a lengthier look at the nature of the need that I see, in principle, for a fixed-rate system, and also at the reasons why, conversely, it seems to me persuasive even on purely theoretical grounds that a flexible-rate system would undermine rather than encourage marketplace adjustments.

In much of the conventional discussion of these issues, there has too often been a tendency to concede a theoretical case for flexible rates as a counterpart of the flexibility that characterizes a market economy. I am not that congenial. Moreover, after I have outlined my reasons for challenging the case for flexible rates on broadly theoretical grounds, I intend to go further to describe some of the practical considerations that would render a system of flexible rates unworkable, even if there were good theoretical grounds for making the attempt. And beyond the generally applicable constraints of realism, there are also the direct and special needs of the United States. I make no apologies for regarding these, too, as crucial, and so will add to my general list of operational obstacles some mention of the unique disadvantages that a flexible rate system would impose on the United States.

There is still a further and final set of considerations, however, which must also be faced frankly. For even though we might agree that a system of fixed exchange rates is clearly preferable on theoretical grounds, and even though it is clearly a much more workable system for the world as a whole, and for the United States, we do have to ask whether some other kind of fatal flaw might yet develop in the structure of the fixed exchange rate system—a crack in the structure that could require its abandonment. Specifically, a fixed-rate system needs a gradually increasing supply of internationally usable monetary reserves. Is there a risk that the world will run out of acceptable monetary reserves; that the countries of the world, taken together, cannot add to their holdings of reserves fast enough, as world trade grows, to support their own exchange rates on a fixed standard through alternating periods of relative strength or weakness for one country after another? If the fixed exchange rate system is inexorably headed for this kind of collapse, because there are not enough reserves to go around for an expanding world economy, then we might by default have to fall back on a system of flexible exchange rates, despite the forbidding shortcomings of that system.

My concluding comments will suggest that a satisfactory answer can and will be found. Indeed, perhaps paradoxically, I suspect it will be an answer reminiscent of some of Professor Friedman's other writings. Not the answer of flexible rates, but instead I expect that the countries of the world will initiate for their global reserve needs some version of that proposal for a regular and continuing creation of money that has so long been identified, for the needs of domestic economies, with Professor Friedman's name. But before getting to that, there is much other intervening ground that I must cover. First, a brief sketch of what I think is meant conceptually by a fixed-rate system, in contrast with one consisting of "free" or flexible exchange rates.

WHAT ARE FIXED EXCHANGE RATES?

Under a system of fixed exchange rates, each country defines a parity for its own currency that is, if I may be unambiguously clear, neither rigidly fixed nor freely flexible. Moreover, a number of countries—ordinarily including some that are less developed, and others that are going through a radical transition of some kind—will set no parity at all.

What all of this does mean, though, is a system which presumes that a central core of leading countries, through whom most of the trade and payments move, will each set a parity for its own currency; that these parities will be defined in terms of some commonly accepted standard or norm, such as the dollar; and that cross rates can consequently be calculated among these various currencies for determining with fair accuracy how many Japanese yen, for example, would be equivalent to one Swedish kroner, or one Mexican peso. There can, around these parities, be some moderate fluctuation, such as the plus-or-minus 1 percent permitted by the International Monetary Fund for countries that have declared a parity to the Fund, have met certain other criteria, and are prepared freely to buy or sell their own currency at prices within that band.

Any of these countries, too, on proper notice to the Fund can actually alter their own declared parity (making up to the IMF for any losses that it might otherwise suffer on its own holdings of that currency, in the event the change in parity is a devaluation). Those who use the currency of such a country—individuals, firms, or nations—may possibly take out protection against a devaluation, for example, by making certain they owe some debts in a vulnerable currency to offset their claims denominated in that currency. Or they may avoid commitments in suspect currencies by trying to get much of their business with such countries denominated and payable in a universally usable currency, such as United States dollars. Or, in the case of about one-half dozen of the leading countries, they may be able actually to "hedge" by selling short in the forward markets that are maintained in these few currencies by specialized foreign exchange traders.

There will also be other countries which have not declared a parity. Their monetary authorities make their own rules for buying and selling their own currency in terms of some universal standard, such as the United States dollar. But there is a general presumption, in a world that is "on" a fixed exchange rate system, that these countries will, when their own conditions show some reasonable stability and strength, establish a parity of their own. Meanwhile, these non-parity countries, as well as the traders, investors, and bankers of every country, can conduct their daily affairs with the convertible countries in the comfortable assurance that changes of any serious magnitude in those currencies will be quite unusual, and ordinarily preceded and highlighted by special circumstances which prompt users of any such currency to take special precautions. That is, most of the time, though with a wary eye for the occasional exception, anyone can assume that the yardstick for measuring values among the leading countries, and calculating in different currencies the prices of the products which they buy or sell, has on it a fixed scale.

The undergirding of the fixed exchange rate system

is its common reference point, into which all parities can be readily translated. Though one might perhaps imagine others, the one we now have, which has the sanction of time, usage, and universal recognition, is the dollar price of gold. This is not the place, at least not yet, to debate the gold price issue or the gold policy of the United States. But I should make clear that the fixed-rate system, as presently conceived, does presume a fixed price of gold. The parities of other currencies may be expressed in terms of dollars, but that of the dollar is in terms of gold.

The alternative system, that of free or flexible rates, has presumably already been thoroughly described here by Professor Friedman. Subject to correction after I learn what he said, I need only make a few definitional comments. I do not want to quibble over some of the so-called middle-ground proposals. The notion of a slightly wider band for spot-rate fluctuations around parity, say to 2 or even 3 percent, I am going to leave aside. Similarly, at least in these prepared remarks, I will not discuss the suggestions for slow but frequent and regular increases in the gold price. Both are essentially, I think, rooted in acceptance of what I consider the fundamental advantages of a fixed-rate system. My principal question about them is whether, in trying to help strengthen the functioning of that system, they introduce too many new hazards of the kind that I see in a fully flexible system. To be brief and blunt about it, in my view, the wider band idea might someday be of some use; the incremental gold price change would be an unmitigated disaster.

The crucial issues concerning the nature of the world's monetary system really come into focus in a contrast between the kind of fixed-rate world I have just sketched and one in which no country attempts to set a parity for its currency. In the purest formulation of a "free-rate" world, a market springs up for the exchange of currencies, and changing quotations for those currencies are produced by supply and demand forces from hour to hour. The market may have many locations, but presumably active arbitrage and rapid communication among centers will produce a consistent set of quotations almost anywhere at any time. Even in this system, convenience would dictate use of one or a very few currencies as the common denominator, or unit of account. And the rates of most smaller countries would be expressed almost exclusively in terms of only one or two of the leading currencies.

In this rather rarified kind of truly "free" system, there would be no intervention in the foreign exchange market, and no action directly impinging on that market, by the central bank of any country. I leave it for Professor Friedman to say whether this means that there could not, in turn, be any central bank anywhere that could take discretionary action to affect the money supply of its own domestic economy; but I suspect that in a rigorous analysis this would have to be the case. At any rate, because I feel happier when the dancing angels are brought down from the head of a pin on to solid ground, I do not propose to spend very much time with the "pure" version.

For most of what I shall try to say during these debates, I will be talking not about "free" exchange rates—the romantically appealing term used in the title set for this program—but about "fluctuating" or "flexible" exchange rates. That is a system in which, broadly speaking, there are no parities for any currency and the exchange rate of any country is expected to decline whenever its aggregate outpayments exceed its inpayments, to rise when its inpayments are the larger, and to steady out when external payments are back in balance. Short-lived erratic influences, it is assumed (and I stress, *assumed*), would be smoothed out by active spot and forward markets for all, or virtually all, currencies. Central banks would be presumed to exist, but any intervention by them in the exchange markets should be quite limited —mainly to offset any misleading effects of their own domestic actions that might otherwise obscure the underlying supply and demand situation.

Having worked the idealized versions of both the fixed and the flexible systems down somewhat closer to earthy reality, I now feel more comfortable about asking how they compare in terms of principle. After a look at that question, I will move on to more operational considerations.

THEORETICAL ASPECTS OF BOTH SYSTEMS

Both systems rest on the premise that money should serve trade, and that the best money system is one which serves not just passively but also constructively—that is, it not merely assures the availability of an adequate means of payment, but also helps to provide a climate for confident expansion of the economy and for the most productive allocation of resources. The differences between the two systems show up in the way they might be expected to work for the ordinary businessman and banker; in the way in which they might affect the pattern of payments flows among countries; in their differing impacts on the mechanism for balance-of-payments adjustment among countries; and more broadly in their implications for the flourishing expansion of trade in the world economy over the years.

Under a fixed-rate system, there is an established scale of measurement, easily translatable from one country to another, which enables the merchants, investors, and bankers of any one country to do business with others on known terms. The flexible-rate system cannot offer that kind of assurance. No single trader can know enough about all the developments likely to affect the rate of exchange between his own country and that of his client to make a firm contract without including a substantial allowance for the risk that the rate of exchange between the currencies involved will change while the transaction is underway. Prices in international trade and the costs of doing international business of any kind would thus almost inevitably become higher under a flexible-rate system—higher because the businessman must include a charge for the added element of risk.

The customary reply of the "flexible rate school" is not, in fact, an answer. Members of this school do correctly point out that an exchange rate fixed at a disequilibrium level is also bad for trade and adjustment; but as I have already stressed, individual rates (with the exception of the United States, as further described later on) can and should be changed when there is a persisting disequilibrium under a fixed-rate system. But there is also, under a fixed system, a two-way function of established rates—that is, oftentimes the stability of a rate provides the framework for a useful shifting of supply and demand relationships into a settled equilibrium, just as, at much less frequent times, imbalances between the supply and demand for a currency may require a change in the fixed rate itself. Moreover, the obligation to maintain a fixed rate can often provide a country with the needed incentive for carrying through internal adjustments that are vitally needed on purely domestic grounds.

But the further reply of the "flexible raters," with respect to the potential burden of rate instability or fluctuations upon the costs of doing international business, is that the banks or other foreign exchange traders can easily generalize the cost of any uncertainty, and in effect "average it out," by maintaining an active forward market in all of the currencies. Then the trader can pay a known and minimal cost for obtaining forward "cover" for his risk of exchange-rate fluctuation. To be sure, a full-scale organization of foreign exchange markets may help minimize the overall cost of this kind of hedging. But the task of "making" a market in currency futures when there are no known par values is much more complicated than the operations of the futures trader in a single commodity. When expectations about the future performance of a given country, and in turn about the strength of its currency, all begin to run in one direction, where—in the absence of some clear signal from monetary authorities who might be prepared to intervene—do the proponents of flexible rates expect to find private underwriters to make forward markets, except perhaps at costs which any foreign trader would have to consider excessive?

Under a flexible-rate system, the trader must try to take into account the whole range of prospective future payments from and to the particular country for goods and services of every kind, as well as all manner of capital movements, and various states of mind. Nor can the relatively small per annum charges made by the futures traders of today's fixed-rate system be projected into the conditions of a fluctuating rate system. For today's futures traders work against known parities, not an unknown array of unknowables, and they often operate within spread ranges that are protected by central bank intervention. Moreover, the very limits set by the margins for spot-rate fluctuation do, as I can testify from considerable experience, tend by themselves to limit (though admittedly in a somewhat elastic way) the range of forward-rate movements—even without central bank intervention directly in the forward market itself. Yet even with all this shelter, the very aggressive and competitive community of foreign exchange dealers in the world today only maintains active and reliable forward markets in about a half dozen of the world's strongest and most widely used currencies.

Moreover, the burden of the risk premium on trade and other payments is only the first of several comparative disadvantages of the flexible-rate system. Another comes in the distorting influence exerted upon the composition and pattern of payments flows among countries. For as mentioned earlier, one other form of "hedging" against the exchange risk on any given set of payments to or from a country is to have a debt transaction of about the same magnitude running in the opposite direction. So with or without active forward markets, business firms of all kinds will have a compelling inducement to buy from the countries in which they sell, and financial institutions to incur debts to match their claims in each country. To be sure, that kind of bilateral pairing, by firms and by countries, will not always be manageable, but what I am stressing is the ominous significance of a system which inherently generates strong inducements of this kind. They work exactly opposite from the presumed objectives of a market economy, which should be to encourage an environment in which everyone may be able to sell or buy, or borrow or lend, wherever the gain from each transaction can be maximized.

Problems of this kind, added to the sheer wear and tear of trying to do business with a rubber yardstick for a measure, would not only be deterrents to the spread of diversification across national frontiers but actually would, I am convinced, contribute to a greater economic isolationism. A wall of currency uncertainty would be built around every country. What this means is that the inducement to bilateralize foreign trade would be accompanied by a further inducement to trade at home, within the area over which one's own currency can be freely used (that is, where exchange-rate fluctuations are automatically avoided).

Granting all these dampening influences on the long-run expansion of multilateralized world trade that would come with a flexible-rate system, might it still be possible that gains of another kind could more than offset these losses? What about the widely discussed need for improvement in the balance-of-payments adjustment mechanism? If a replacing of fixed rates with flexible rates could assure a more effective and less disruptive procedure for bringing the balance of payments of various countries into viable relationships with each other, then perhaps the price of some dampening in the growth of total trade might be well worth paying. And indeed, a rather impressive case has at times been made that the post-World War II premises of economic life now leave exchange rates as the only usable variable for achieving adjustment flexibility. For wages, and prices, and employment within a country can no longer, it is plausibly argued, be reduced in order to improve the country's trading position abroad—that is, deliberately induced slack is simply not acceptable as the way for a country to "adjust" itself into a position of overall balance or surplus in its payments to and from other countries.

I certainly recognize that this is, when put starkly in these terms, the most troublesome dilemma faced by the fixed-rate system. It ignores, however, the role of capital flows in balance-of-payments disequilibrium and in the restoration of equilibrium. And so far as the trade accounts themselves are concerned, my own answer—without questioning the downside rigidity of prices, the persistent upward pressure of wages, or the priority appropriate for sustained employment—is that suitable adjustment can still be accomplished under a fixed-rate system through variations in the rate and pattern of advance. For another premise of postwar political economy is that each country's economy will be dynamic—continually growing, adapting, and changing within a world of rising expectations. The engineering of economic policy may be a little more difficult in such a dynamic world; the analysis must be a little more sophisticated and the policy action a little more delicate; and we do not yet have accumulated patterns of experience to make the judgments easier; but I see no reason conceptually why the same kinds of adjustments cannot now be achieved through variations which merely affect the speed of an economy's forward motion, and the composition of its output, that could earlier have been attempted through deliberate deflation in the days when the world lived on the premises of a relatively static economy. And, of course, with capital markets growing, the opportunities for aggravating, and for offsetting, effects upon the balance of payments from capital flows become increasingly important in qualifying any generalizations made with respect primarily to trade. The same can be said, moreover, concerning transactions on government account.

One difference, at least for some years until the policymakers of the world have more experience to build upon, and a readier acuity for the fine tuning that will occasionally be needed, is that countries facing a need for major adjustment in the structure or pattern of trade will sometimes have to have a longer period to complete necessary adaptations than would have been considered appropriate in earlier years. This means that individual countries in deficit will in some circumstances need access to more reserves—reserves that they own, or reserves that can be borrowed, or both. And countries in surplus will need to accept the implications of surpluses—both in the holding and the using of reserves.

But the essentials of the adjustment process under the fixed-rate system, and now familiar to all countries, can surely remain the same. Loss of reserves, perhaps accompanied by a need to resort to borrowing, will impel a country to look inward upon the performance of its own economy to discover the cause. And if prices are rising rapidly, or wage increases are exceeding productivity, or investment demands are outrunning resources, or the production of salable export crops is being restricted, or government requirements (including overseas spending) are adding undue strain upon total capacity, for example, then appropriate action can be taken, with results that may alter the economy's forward speed for a time, but need not mean general recession and unemployment. Concern over depleting reserves, as well as pressure to repay reserves that have been temporarily borrowed, will under a fixed-rate system provide the balance-of-payments "prod" to carry through such action—even though the need for that action, if not the recognition of the need, could be as great or greater for purely domestic reasons. Reserve gains, in the opposite direction, will be the stimulus to further reduction of trade restrictions, the opening of capital markets to foreign borrowers, the extending of foreign aid or investment, and the expansion of the home market.

This is not the place, and I certainly lack the competence, to digress further into these familiar and tantalizing subjects. I do strongly urge, however, that it is not only possible, but also productive, to resist the easy tendency to see a hopeless conflict between balance-of-payments viability and progressive gain in the domestic economy. Conflict can exist, do not misunderstand me, and not every proposed prescription for balance-of-payments correction under a fixed-rate system would fit the premises of the modern economy. But I am sure there can also be ways of using balance-of-payments signals constructively to meet, in combination, both external and internal needs. The strength and significance of any such signals under a system of flexible rates would, I am afraid, be much weaker.

For the intention, under a flexible-rate system, would be for any country to let its exchange rate against other currencies fall to a new equilibrium position whenever aggregate outpayments exceeded inpayments. In effect, whenever the balance of payments might point to something wrong in the home economy—when the product mix or the savings mix or the investment mix or some other aspects of the domestic economy are out of joint and need correction—the risk is that the exchange rate would simply move to compensate for things the way they are and the correction would be avoided. That might theoretically be all right if balance-of-payments problems were always merely warts on the economic body, quite unrelated to its own functioning, and an annoying nuisance best removed through simple surgery. But, as I would hope you might agree, that is rarely the case.

To be sure, a declining exchange rate itself might be considered sufficient cause for alarm to set corrective domestic economic reactions in motion. But with no norms to defend, and with no pressure from reserve losses or from needed borrowing to reinforce the policymaker's resolve, the likelihood of any corrective reaction pattern is a little hard to predict. Indeed, perhaps the most likely reaction, to take the case of a country experiencing rapid inflation, would be toward accentuation, not containment, of the exchange-rate decline, for the domestic prices of exports could then increase behind the screen of lower exchange costs to foreigners, import costs would rise, wages would no doubt be raised even further, and a new wage floor would have, in effect, been built under the inflation already realized. And given a commitment to flexible rates, it is hard to see where this process would end, except in a sequence of competitive devaluations. That is the kind of chaos experienced in the thirties that the Bretton Woods system was specifically designed to avoid.

The same downside rigidities and upward price drift in our postwar economies that make adjustment more difficult under fixed-exchange rates would, in my view, make for progressive inflation, and successive waves of exchange-rate depreciation from one country to the next, if countries were trying to follow a flexible-rate system. The one telling influence for relative price stability that is universally recognized, if not respected, in today's world is that exerted by a country's balance-of-payments position. A flexible-rate system permits a country to cut itself off from the international force of market competition—the greatest defender the world now has for protecting the stability of domestic monetary values.

Moreover, I am really puzzled over what could happen to the allocation of capital among and within countries, over time, with exchange rates fluctuating frequently and at times widely. Often, indeed, those differentials in interest rates and profits that help to bring capital to its most productive uses would simply be offset. The mere beginning of the capital flows themselves might set off exchange-rate adjustments that would bottle up any further flows, or if not, the exchange risks might well exceed the potential interest or dividend gain. And as I mentioned earlier, this could mean that capital flows to any particular country would be roughly limited to the amount of corresponding obligations that one could obtain as a hedge in that same country or currency. By contrast, a fixed-rate system, for all its imperfections, does provide a reasonably stable set of benchmarks within which long-range capital commitments can be planned and worked out in terms of calculated profitability.

But I must not go on any longer with this list of the shortcomings of a flexible-rate system as seen from the theoretical side. What it all comes down to is that the economic traffic among nations has become too vast and too complex—including raw materials and processed goods, services, and all forms and maturities of capital—for me, at least, to be able to conceive of any satisfactory way in which a system of fluctuating rates could really determine the rates that people need to use from day to day. Individual foreign exchange traders and bankers would have an almost impossible task in groping for a going rate that could take all of these conflicting influences into account. Their task would be similar to, though larger than, that of various individuals attempting to come up with a firm figure for the wholesale or retail price index of a country, for example, and then being prepared to write contracts on the basis of an unofficial pooling of each other's estimates. I am very much afraid that the rate for any currency against all others would have to fluctuate so widely that the country's own trade would be throttled and its capital misdirected. But that leads directly into the next area of difficulty. Thus far we have been talking in terms of the theory of what either system might attempt to do. Now I want to turn for a little while to actual operating considerations.

OPERATIONAL ISSUES

The hard fact is, I am convinced, that no country able to control its own exchange rate will in practice allow it to float. Even if flexible in form, the exchange rate of any such country is going to be watched over by the financial authorities of that country. That is to say, even if a compelling theoretical case could be made for "flexible" rates among countries—and you have seen that I do not think it can—the same forces that have given us the downward rigidities of prices, wages, and employment in this postwar era would impel the government and central bank of any reasonably developed country to try to control its own exchange rate. For the exchange rate can be a powerful weapon. When settled at a particular level for any country, it determines the comparative costs of all the country's imports and all of its exports. If the entire system were to become unhinged, few countries could as a matter of practical politics stand by and let their rate against other currencies be influenced by the intervention of the authorities of the other countries without at least taking some defensive action.

The practical answer to the natural wish of each country to gain the apparent advantage of a slightly undervalued currency has had to be the kind of armed truce provided by a fixed-rate system, which allows only narrow margins for market-rate fluctuation in response to shifting supply and demand conditions. All of that is now given status through the par-value procedures of the International Monetary Fund. And whenever the price and wage structure of a country is persistently out of line, the country may, of course, change its parity, though even then only under the watchful and appraising eyes of all other members of the Fund.

The alternative opportunity that would be opened by a worldwide system of flexible rates would, I very much fear, be a continuous invitation to economic warfare as countries maneuvered their rates against each other—or more charitably, influenced their own rates to reflect in each case the immediate interest of the country concerned. There then would be no widely recognized, established rate levels, and no presumption of any obligation to maintain rate stability. The advantage of being able to sell abroad a little cheaper, without necessarily lowering domestic prices, would always make "just a little more" depreciation attractive. Countries would simply be unable to leave their rates alone. And without such abstinence, whatever may have been claimed as the theoretical advantages of a flexible-rate system would in practice surely be dissipated, if not lost.

Every foreign exchange trader whom I know, including to be sure the traders of most of the central banks of the leading countries, has at one time or another told me in puzzlement that he has never been able to visualize the operational arrangements that could prevail under a flexible-rate system. Nor can I. None of us is able to imagine that any private traders, or groups of traders, could have the courage or capacity to make markets in all currencies, or even only in the major currencies, without some benchmarks to guide them. That is one impelling reason why I think it inevitable that every central bank will always have to be a factor of some importance in the market trading of its own currency against others —if not through active intervention, then at least through the setting of a par value and buying or selling at the outer limits of the agreed margin for variation around that par value.

Moreover, without the underlying steadiness afforded by an official presence (or some official participation) in the spot market, I doubt that forward markets could ever as a practical matter get started in any currencies—except perhaps at discounts so large as to make the nominal markets meaningless, if not ridiculous. And yet the existence of forward markets for virtually all currencies is usually given as a prerequisite for the functioning of a flexible-rate system in all of the theoretical discussions.

Nor can one forget the need for people to perform the functions of dealers and traders. While the little coterie of foreign exchange practitioners certainly does not include all who might have talent for this occult art, it is an open society which anyone with a trading knack is welcome to enter. Talent in this field seems always, in fact, to enjoy a sellers' market. Yet it must be significant that I have never met anyone who has attained the competence of a seasoned trader who would be prepared to continue in the business if, by some sleight of hand, all parities were to be abandoned and the central banks were barred from entering the markets in their own currencies. Many, and I include myself, would probably want to withdraw from trading activities even under the sort of flexible-rate system in which the central banks were allowed a role, so long as there were no parity guidelines to get us into the right ball park. At any rate, so far as forward trading is concerned, if I had no parity guidelines in the spot market, I would certainly not want to be crunched between the pressures generated by central banking giants in a free-for-all. They would be pursuing aims and using tactics, in jockeying rates against each other, that I simply could not interpret in the minute-by-minute environment that makes a trading market.

Mind you, I am not trying to confront Professor Friedman with an organized strike of my fellow traders in the foreign exchange markets of the world, but I do submit that there surely would, even if all of my other objections could be overcome, be no little recruiting problem in getting the trading desks capably manned for a launching of his system.

SPECIAL SITUATION OF UNITED STATES

In addition to the considerations that make flexible rates undesirable and unworkable for most of the world's more advanced countries, there are further problems that would center on the United States. To be sure, because of its dominating size in world trade, and because of the widespread use of dollars as a "currency of convenience" for the international transactions of other countries, the United States will inevitably have unique problems as well as unique opportunities under any system of international monetary arrangements. Its central role in the system of fixed-exchange rates has superimposed upon the conventional balance-of-payments problems ordinarily encountered by any industrialized country a vulnerability to monetary disturbances or pressures of many kinds from many sources outside the United States. Some of the hazards and burdens related to these pressures will be described shortly, when I try to review with you some of the additional reforms that are going to be needed in order to keep the present fixed-rate system functioning effectively over the years and decades ahead. At this point, though, I want to focus on a number of added risks or strains that would be imposed on the United States if the world were to switch over to a flexible-rate system.

The most significant overall point to be recognized is that the United States can never expect, as a practical matter, to bring about at its own initiative any effective change in its exchange rate vis-à-vis the other countries of the world. This is a consequence of our size and the world's need for use of the dollar as a "vehicle" currency. For us to attempt to initiate a change in our rate against other countries, under a fixed-rate system, or to expect a change to develop to our advantage under a flexible-rate system, is to reverse the natural laws of gravity and magnetism in the monetary system. Any change originating in the United States will in turn be evaluated by all other countries who will then, under either a fixed- or flexible-rate system, take offsetting action to defend themselves.

There is always the possibility, of course, that a system-wide change in parities could be made simultaneously against gold under the present fixed-rate system, or that under a flexible-rate system the gold price might fluctuate frequently—with uniform consequences for all currencies in either case. Yet to change the gold price for the system as a whole, under the fixed-rate system, would undermine confidence for the future in the stabilizing central point of reference to which all other elements of the system are hinged. It cannot be considered by the responsible governments of the leading countries. Under a flexible system, frequent changes in the price of gold would only be another manifestation of the built-in uncertainties which would weaken the reliance that businessmen and bankers could then place on the continuity of any monetary values.

Aside from a change in the price of gold—which is the one way that might be theoretically considered for exerting a uniform change in the value of all currencies—the interesting and relevant questions concern instead the kinds of changes that might in fact occur in the exchange rates among countries. Having already noted that the United States cannot effectively maintain rates designed for its own advantage, vis-à-vis the outside world as a whole, I should also stress that it nonetheless can be the source of changes which will then subsequently be more precisely tuned by the individual countries on the other end of the pairing (i.e., between the dollar and each of the other currencies).

The additional hazards for the United States under a flexible-rate system come mainly from the fact that dollars are widely used a vehicle currency, and consequently may be held in transactions balances in larger or smaller amounts by the businessmen, investors, and bankers of other countries. This inevitably means a special kind of exposure for the United States, as well as giving us the opportunity to serve as bankers for much of the world.

We have certainly not yet worked out an easy accommodation to the exposure aspect of this unavoidable opportunity. But we have, under the fixed-rate system, been able to minimize the purely speculative capital flows, and to neutralize the impact of all such flows on the reserve position of the United States—so long as the causes are temporary. Where the causes are lasting, there are consequences in long-term capital flows and adjustments that we are learning to recognize. But the overriding point is this: whatever has been accomplished has come about only because the central banks and the private markets have created new facilities within the framework provided by a set of fixed parities among the leading countries. And changes in those parities, as in the cases of France, Germany, the Netherlands, and Canada during the past decade, for example, have been made as discrete steps, within a structure of assurances that rates were going to be kept in place, once declared.

But the exposure that the United States must face would be magnified under a flexible-rate system. As if earlier conditions would not have made those risks grave enough, the development in recent years of the so-called Euro-dollar market, in which deposits of many billions of dollars are held on the books of foreign banks, has greatly enlarged the scale of such problems. I am not even talking here about the ways in which shifts of these Euro-dollar funds may affect the different methods of accounting for our balance of payments. What matters most for this discussion is that there now can be, in magnitudes much larger than anything experienced in the past, massive movements into dollars from other currencies, or out of dollars back into other currencies—shifts that can amount to several billions of dollars within a few days, or even hours. Under a system of flexible rates, shifts of this kind (which have now become commonplace, and for which we now do have a variety of effective cushioning devices to minimize or neutralize possible disturbing side effects) would be expected to work themselves out entirely in changes in the exchange rate.

The consequences of these movements of volatile funds could not, under a flexible-rate system, be cushioned by a network of forward-market transactions; they are much too large and capricious for that. Instead, they would have to be reflected in changes in the spot rates themselves—changes that would inevitably have the same effect as changes in the terms of trade between the United States and all other countries. Thus, when the net flow might be inward into additional dollars, the exchange rate for the dollar would rapidly strengthen against other currencies. American importers would find that the prices of foreign goods had suddenly become much cheaper for them, provided they could quickly complete transactions through the immediate purchase of the needed foreign currencies. And conversely, American exporters would find a sudden decline in their sales contracts. As soon as the flow into dollars ceased, quite apart from the further effect of a reverse flow, the rate would necessarily decline, the importing fall back, the exporting become more competitive, and if this same whip-sawing had not occurred too often in the recent past, the merchants engaged in foreign trade might try to resume more normal business. But the costs in physical adjustment—or in forward cover where that could possibly be arranged—would place such a strain on the merchants engaged in foreign trade that only the hardiest could survive at all.

To be sure, the enlarged potential for shifts into and out of dollars that has been generated by the development of the Euro-dollar market only enlarges the scale of problems that have often been recognized, in discussions of a flexible-rate system, when consideration was given to the possible impact of short-term capital movements on changes in exchange rates. There is no question, in my mind, that the unusual exposure of the United States to this type of hazard would have results that could be completely disruptive to the orderly conduct of our commercial trade.

The argument has been made at times that flexible rates could work well for one or two industrialized countries, so long as all of the other countries maintained a fixed set of exchange-rate relationships. The most notable case, of course, was that of Canada until 1962. There it was often argued that movements of short-term capital produced a change in the exchange rate against the United States dollar that was equilibrating, helping in turn to achieve a balance between inpayments and outpayments without the need for extensive use of Canada's monetary reserves. While that history will long be studied and re-studied, and argued and re-argued, my own feeling is that even in that very special case, the avoidance of reserve strains, as changes occurred in the structural relations between Canada and the United States, lulled Canada into a false sense of security. In the end, it became necessary for Canada to establish a fixed parity for its dollar. But by that time, the problems of internal structural realignment then confronting Canada were much more difficult, at least as I see the situation, than might have been the case if Canada had been maintaining the trade and investment patterns consistent with a fixed exchange rate and intermittent swings in foreign exchange reserves over the years. Even so, the test is a poor one because, either through influencing the interest rates that affected capital flows between our two countries, or by affecting the exchange rate itself, the Canadian authorities were certainly not standing aside, to permit the full range of possible rate fluctuation.

It is this inevitability of intervention by the monetary authorities of other countries, whenever they see capital flows or trade moving significantly against them, that makes the position of the United States so peculiarly vulnerable under a flexible-rate system. And in turn, the exchange-rate fluctuations that will be generated, not only by market forces but by official intervention, can certainly be expected, at least some of the time, to generate destabilizing additional movements of short-term capital.

I am quite aware that this description of the extra strains that a flexible-rate system would impose on the United States runs counter to the picture described by Professor Friedman in his testimony before the Joint Economic Committee in November, 1963, when he implied that the United States could have been insulated from what he called "enormous power [given] to officials of foreign governments" by our balance-of-payments deficits. I can certainly overlook his characterization of my own efforts at that time as a "frantic search for expedients." But I have never been able to understand how he could argue that we would have been spared any balance-of-payments strain, and our domestic economy kept completely insulated, if only our exchange rate against all other countries had been free in those circumstances to decline. For that was the period, you will remember, when the first of a series of measures had to be introduced to help check the tumbling outflow of American capital, both long term and short term. The momentum of those outflows, in a flexible-rate environment, would undoubtedly have produced so sharp a decline in our exchange rate against other countries that American exporters would have had a field day. And I have little doubt that the monetary authorities of other countries, seeing an impending avalanche of American goods would promptly have taken offsetting action to adjust their own exchange rates and return the relative relations closer to the level that might have originally prevailed. But even if I should be wrong in that presumption, the result then actually would have been a tremendous stimulus for American exports, a sharp rise in the price of our imports, an all-around sequence of other internal cost and wage increases, and the initiation of internal inflationary pressures that would have quite upset the relative price stability which was doing so much, at that time, to help create the conditions for an improvement of productivity and the orderly growth of the American economy.

I realize, of course, that meditations of this kind on the history of "what might have been," are no more than personal daydreams. But I do submit that they are at least as credible, as descriptions of the potentials of a flexible-rate system in 1963, as those which Professor Friedman adduced in his testimony.

Moreover, having reflected on his characterization of the impact that a flexible-rate system might have had in these circumstances, I find it hard to reconcile the kinds of advantages he claims in these circumstances with the description that he gives of a flexible-rate system at other times. For he has also said something else. In attempting to defend a flexible system against the charge (which I have certainly been making here) that exchange rates would often fluctuate widely, with harmful consequences for the volume and the composition of trade, he has asserted that the expected result should ordinarily be a relatively stable pattern of rates. He wrote in his classic essay on "The Case for Flexible Exchange Rates" that "advocacy of flexible exchange rates is *not* equivalent to advocacy of unstable exchange rates. The ultimate objective is a world in which exchange rates, while *free* to vary, are in fact highly stable." It is that stability, and its advantages as well as its shortcomings, which I think best serves the interests of the United States—but I do not see how Professor Friedman can have it both ways.

A FATAL FLAW?

One advantage that I have in this debate is that I am defending the essentials of the system that is already in place. But, I can already hear the murmur, "What a system!" And I must agree that it is far from perfect. Nonetheless, I do have the comfort of knowing that it does actually work. And I have the conviction, born of some bias as well as some experience, that most of the harsh and unsettling aspects of the working of this system, as they have been most conspicuous most recently in the United Kingdom, are very largely man-made and can be man-corrected within the premises of a fixed-rate system. All of us are learning through the years what can be helpful in reducing the anguish while enjoying the achievements which this system generates.

There is, however, one emerging problem in the functioning of a fixed-rate system that is so fundamental that I must frankly concede that the system could disintegrate if that problem is not carefully diagnosed and

resolved within the next few years. I am not going to
wander off into the many other kinds of improvements
that could be visualized to make the system work more
effectively, nor will I try here to describe the further
implications for our own domestic economic policy in
the United States that are, at least to my eye, being so
clearly signaled by our present balance-of-payments
deficits. I do want to conclude with a few comments
and suggestions on this crucial fault which, if it widens
much further before it is corrected, could bring the
system down. Should that happen, I suspect the result
would be a world divided into smaller trading blocs,
enjoying the advantages of fixed exchange rates within
each bloc and the hardships of barter between blocs—
rather than any turn toward Professor Friedman's flexible-rate system. But perhaps we can argue about that
next week.

What threatens to undermine the fixed-rate system
now is the fact that the supply of gold, the ultimate
reserve on which the system depends, cannot be expected
to grow rapidly enough in world monetary reserves to
provide the primary liquidity that the countries will
need for making settlements among themselves at fixed
rates of exchange. Up until now, it has been possible to
build upon gold another kind of primary reserve, first
in the form of British pounds sterling, then for more
limited areas the French franc, the Dutch guilder, and
others, and then on a worldwide scale, the United States
dollar. In principle, this is the way—the supplying of

usable national currencies—in which an adequate answer can be found for meeting the world's growing reserve needs as the world's scale of economic activities expands.

The reason that this need cannot simply be solved by a change in the price of gold is very similar to the reason why the world cannot effectively function on a flexible-rate system. In my view, the premise for an effective functioning of a market economy, guided by changes in relative prices, is that the numeraire must remain relatively constant. That is why, as I see it, we need a fixed-rate system. For in the developed world, at any rate, we simply face an unresolvable problem in which there are more unknowns than there are variables, once we introduce fluctuations in the unit of measurement itself which may be so large or so capricious that a stable resolution of all the forces cannot be found. The unit of measurement must remain reasonably constant (in the sense of predictability) in order that all other elements can move up and down in a measurable, and thus meaningful, way. The alternatives, for the world as a whole—though individual countries may go otherwise so long as the leading countries do not—is surely either barter or exchange control, introducing another kind of certainty into the measurement of relationships. Without the temerity to attempt a mathematical demonstration of a point that most eminent mathematical economists apparently do not accept, I can at least suggest the need for further scientific testing of a hypothesis that the whole world of finance and trade now lives by.

It is just as misleading, in my view, to think that the external value of a currency can be determined in some detached way by fluctuating supply and demand as it is to think that the price of gold can be varied frequently without weakening its usefulness as a standard of value. Instead, just as the supply of money for individual nations must be man-made, within a framework of arrangements that aims at maintaining stable values, so the supply of gold at the base of the world's monetary system must be augmented by new arrangements. In effect, while preserving the fixed price, those arrangements would add a common currency to the gold supply, through the combined action and commitment of a number of countries, acting together. The world would not then, henceforth, have to rely primarily on the issuance of one currency to provide the acceptable supplement to gold.

The need, in effect, in order to preserve the $35 price as the kingpin of the whole structure of fixed exchange rates, while providing for regular and controlled increases in the supply of gold for reserve purposes, is to find an effective and convincing method for creating the equivalent of additional gold. That is the object of the international monetary discussions which have now been under way for more than three years. This is no simple matter. Countries will have to make lasting commitments to contribute to the creation of, and to accept and hold and use, a new kind of international money that rests upon the joint and several obligations of all of them.

Such obligations cannot be undertaken lightly. They demand from each country a careful search of the risk that its own direct interests may at some time be jeopardized by these arrangements. It is small wonder, then, that much time has been consumed in working toward agreed principles of operation, long after the stage has been reached of preliminary agreement on the need for planning of this kind.[1]

I feel certain that the members of the International Monetary Fund will, in what still may be many months but will be less than many years, find a way to agree on prudent methods for creating what Secretary [Frederick L.] Deming, [Under Secretary of the Treasury for Monetary Affairs] has called, in a spirit of wholesome compromise, a "Drawing Unit Reserve Asset." I would suggest that his "DURA" be re-christened "DURA-GOLD." It will be an asset that central banks can readily accept and contentedly hold—transferable, usable for obtaining the dollars needed for trading in the foreign exchange markets, and counted as part of each country's primary monetary reserves.

My certainty that a way will be found springs from my conviction that most of the countries of the world want to keep and improve the present environment for a multilateral expansion of trade and investment—the environment among the countries on fixed exchange rates which has made possible in this past decade the greatest expansion of capacity and output that has been achieved by any group of countries at any time. They will be impelled to find an answer because they cannot accept either of the alternatives—the anarchy of an entire world on flexible exchange rates, or (and this would be the more probable) the protectionism and economic autarchy of the sort of currency blocs that prevailed in the 1930s.

REBUTTALS

MILTON FRIEDMAN

Dr. Roosa regards as a key disadvantage of free exchange rates the likelihood that they will exert a dampening influence on world trade and will promote bilateralism and autarchy.

I regard as a key advantage of free exchange rates the likelihood that they will lead to freer world trade, will promote a dismantling of exchange controls and import quotas and a reduction of tariffs.

How can two knowledgeable men reach such diametrically opposed conclusions on this, as on other aspects, of free versus fixed exchange rates?

Needless to say, I believe that my conclusions are correct. So I shall look for defects in Dr. Roosa's arguments, not my own, to explain the conflict. After all, we both believe in division of labor according to comparative advantage, so I can surely leave the defects in my argument to his capable hands.

The explanation, I believe, is that Dr. Roosa applies a double standard. The advantages that he cites for fixed rates are valid and important advantages of a real gold standard, of a unified currency system in which there are no central banks to interfere with the effects of balance-of-payments flows on the quantity of money. Such a standard does weld the world together, does promote international trade, does impose an effective and reasonably mild discipline on internal policies.

If I had to choose between such a standard and a system of national currencies linked by flexible exchange rates, I might very well choose the gold standard, despite the waste of resources involved in digging out gold in one part of the world to bury it in another.

But a real gold standard bears as little relation to the existing system of pegged exchange rates, if I may quote my ex-chancellor, as football does to a college education. Yet, Dr. Roosa discusses the existing system as if it were a real gold standard.

Do pegged rates really provide international traders with certainty when they do not know whether they will be able to convert their exchange a year hence? Or whether they will be able to get import permits? Or whether they will be faced by different pegged rates?

Dr. Roosa recognizes the problem but then resolves it by bland faith. "What about the . . . balance-of-payments adjustment mechanism?" he asks. "I see no reason conceptually," he answers, "why . . . adjustments cannot . . . be achieved through variations which merely affect the speed of an economy's forward motion."

"I am sure," he goes on, "there can also be ways of using balance-of-payment signals constructively to meet, in combination, both external and internal needs."

Perhaps so, but do we know these ways? There is not the slightest sign in his paper that we do. I rubbed my eyes as I read all of this. Do we really have an interest-equalization tax? And is it really being proposed to double it? Is there a "voluntary" credit restraint program? Is there a "voluntary" program to restrict foreign investment? Are there oil import quotas? Has the tourist duty-free allowance been reduced?

Have Japan and Hong Kong been pressured to impose voluntary export quotas? Does Britain have exchange control? Has Germany taken measures to restrict the import of capital?

And so on and on, or are all of these only figments of my overheated imagination induced by my inability to rejoice in the expansion of multilateral world trade with ever-fewer restrictions and impediments?

In Dr. Roosa's story, the discipline of fixed rates is always in the direction of desirable internal policies.

Has Germany not existed these past years? Is it my imagination that fixed rates forced Germany to inflate?

In short, when Dr. Roosa considers fixed exchange rates, he implicitly considers not our actual system but a glittering gold man with only an occasional side glance at the reality it conceals.

When he comes to free exchange rates, he also considers not the system as it would actually operate, compared with the alternatives to it actually available, but

a hypothetical system. This time, however, the hypothetical system is not a gold man but a straw man, a
scarecrow of shreds and patches to frighten children
with. There is none of that bland faith that somehow
methods will be found to cope with possible weaknesses.

No, this time everything is for the worst in the worst
of all possible worlds.

Free rates, Roosa apparently believes, are subject to
Murphy's law, which I am sure you all know. It goes,
"If anything can go wrong, it will." Let me illustrate,
and I quote. "Prices in international trade and the costs
of doing international business of any kind would . . .
almost inevitably become higher under a flexible-rate
system" because of "the added element of risk."

What added element of risk? Compared with a real
gold standard, yes. Compared with a system of pegged
rates, held together by exchange controls, import
quotas, capital restrictions, and occasional changes in
pegged rates? No. Or, at the very least, unproved.

Even more important, as I emphasized in my paper,
under a free rate system some currency or currencies
would undoubtedly become widely used for denominat-
ing international transactions. There need not be even
a presumption of greater risk in such a case.

Or, to look another of the monsters created by Dr.
Roosa's fertile imagination in the face, he conjures up
the possibility that free exchange rates would work
towards "accentuation, not containment" of rapid

inflation. Dr. Roosa envisions that a decline in the exchange rate would mean that the "domestic price of exports could then increase behind the screen of lower exchange costs to foreigners, import costs would rise, wages would no doubt be raised even further," and so on.

This is simply wrong, if free exchange rates are compared with the correct alternative. Suppose the exchange rate is kept pegged despite the inflationary pressure. How can it be kept pegged? Only by controlling imports and exports. But this will make domestic prices of the controlled items differ from their foreign prices. Given the same volume of trade, the domestic prices will be precisely the same under either system.

How does a fixed-rate system provide the country with more resources with which to get more goods than it otherwise could get? Implicitly, again, what Dr. Roosa is doing is to compare the flexible-rate system, not with the actual alternative, but with some hypothetical ideal world in which there is neither exchange rate change nor inflationary pressure.

Dr. Roosa reserves his finest flights of the imagination for the horrors facing exchange traders in spot and forward markets under free exchange rates. I have heard this story before. It is exactly what people said would happen, as I pointed out in my paper, in the housing market before rent control was removed, what people said would happen in Germany in 1948 before price controls were removed. I have little doubt that if we could disinter the files of the Office of Price Administration for 1944 and 1945 we would find a memo explaining the horrible chaos that would follow if price controls and rationing were suddenly removed, producing large and unpredictable fluctuations in prices.

To go farther afield, I am sure that the Gosplan files would reveal dozens of similar memos explaining why a free market could not possibly work under the special conditions of the Soviet Union.

Though Dr. Roosa apparently has unlimited faith in the ability of government bureaucrats to devise sensitive and effective substitutes for market adjustments, he seems to have very little faith in the ability of the market itself to adjust. Like every good administrator, he knows the ins and outs of the present cumbrous system. He knows it works after a fashion and he cannot conceive that there is any other way to run it.

Let me assure him that he will develop a similar expertise in a free exchange rate world and, if only he will let himself go, he would find himself speculating less and enjoying it more. I might add that it's rather curious to find a partner in a major financial house standing here before us and extolling the virtues of government bureaucracy, explaining to us how civil servants can control things fine, while an academician argues that you can't trust those civil servants, you'd better leave it to the private market. But all sorts of strange things happen in this world.

In any event, I must repeat, the world that Dr. Roosa conjures up, the world of bilateral balancing with erratic movements of volatile funds and "fluctuations in the unit of measurement, which may be . . . large . . . or capricious," is a figment of his imagination.

We have had extensive experience with free rates in many countries, including the United States. Let Dr. Roosa show us any empirical case where his fears have been realized, except where there have been initially unstable internal policies. He is a victim of what, in my earlier paper, I called the Arizona effect.

If countries separately follow stable internal policies, exchange rates, while free to move, will be highly stable. Stability is not rigidity.

Finally, I come to Dr. Roosa's comment about the special situation in the United States: "The most significant overall point to be recognized," he writes, "is that the United States can never expect, as a practical matter, to bring about on its own initiative any effective change in its exchange rate vis-à-vis the other countries of the world."

Who ever said it could or should? Certainly not I. I have apparently failed completely to convey to Dr. Roosa my position. So perhaps there is some hope we can still get together.

Would he agree that the United States, could, by itself, do the following four things?

One—Get rid of all elements of exchange control,

direct and indirect.

Two—Announce to the world that it will not try to peg the rate of exchange between the dollar and currencies of other countries.

Three—Announce that it will sell gold to all and sundry at $35 an ounce until its supply runs out or, alternatively, that it will simply stop selling or buying gold.

Four—Proceed to follow a stable internal monetary and fiscal policy designed to foster a reasonably constant price level. (I have my own pet scheme for doing this but, for the present purposes, the broader statement will suffice.)

I find it hard to believe there can be any doubt that the United States by itself can do those four things. Now if it did those four things and other countries chose to tie their currencies to the dollar, fine and dandy. We would then be on the way to a unified currency and Dr. Roosa and I would both be happy.

If, under those circumstances, other countries chose to let their currencies float relative to the dollar, that's also fine and dandy.

If we really followed my Points One and Four, that is, if we really eliminated exchange controls and followed a stable internal policy, we would be on the way to the widespread use of the dollar as an international vehicle currency with other countries able to pursue their own internal policies.

If we did not follow my Point Four, that is if we

did not follow a stable internal policy, some other currency would develop as an international vehicle currency and the rest of the world would at least be insulated against our monetary mistakes and we against theirs.

Under any of these circumstances, those able men who man the emergency telephones in the great central banks and who spend endless hours trying to devise ingenious means whereby everybody can borrow from everybody else without anybody being committed to lend to anyone, those able men could be released to do some truly productive work.

ROBERT V. ROOSA

We both have the same problem. We both think that the other has so glamorized his own world that it has lost contact with the kinds of reality that each of us believes he represents. And I am afraid that unless we can bring these contrasts, as Milton has presented them, down to some closer approximation of an earthy reality we are in danger of spending the evening on opposite sides of a revolving door walking through in opposite directions.

I think we do have to find whether there isn't some way of bringing both of our presentations back to the mainland, back from what he regards, and I regard, as islands of abstraction so remote as to be unrelated to the real potential that the countries of the world now confront.

I think perhaps we will find the beginnings of an answer in the questions that he asks toward the close. In themselves, they help to illustrate the ambitious striving for the ideal which, I believe, characterizes his efforts and colors his judgment as to the potential for achievement.

He asks, just for example, "can the United States get rid of exchange controls?" I'll put it the other way around: Will the United States ever be able to live without its own government having a sense of involvement and responsibility for the rate of exchange between its currency and that of other currencies in the world?

The United States, as I have already explained, isn't going to be able to do very much about its own rate against other currencies, not on its own initiative. But the other countries of the world, and Professor Friedman has indicated he would welcome the kind of development in which this might occur, the other countries of the world are going to have to react continually to the pattern of influences that is generated by conditions in the United States, in setting their exchange rates against the dollar.

And we, here, are certainly never going to be in a position to proceed on the premise that he offers by implication, the premise that we will simply take the exchange rate offered in an environment in which there are no ground rules, in which every other country is free by definition to proceed to the advantages of competitive depreciation, to beggar each other's neighbor, as was done through the thirties, an experience that is all too searing still in our memories to forget and which I do commend to him when he asks whether there is any experience with the sort of approach that he is recommending.

The end result then was a deterioration into currency blocs which became competitive and abrasive to the point of producing bilateralism and the shrinking of trade patterns. I am sure these are inherent when there are no clear ground rules by which countries are guided, and when changes are made in exchange rates in response not only to the trade flow but also to the capital flows that are of overriding importance (and will be) in the determination of the exchange rate of this or any other country under his system.

Or, look at the other question. Can I give him any assurance that the United States will follow a consistent policy aimed at internal stability? I can't.

I can assure him, as I am sure all of you could, that the United States is committed and every free country in the world is committed to a set of objectives—and that their objectives limit Professor Friedman's conditions of pure and idealistic freedom with a number of premises.

Neither the United States government, nor any government, is going to withdraw from responsibility for the maintenance of employment, for providing minimum levels of wages and the acceptance of a downward rigidity both in prices and in wages. These are parts of the real world that I had in mind when I said there is a risk that in trying both to formulate his questions and to imply his answers he is forgetting where it is we live and what it is we are going to have to find a solution for. None of the solutions are going to be simple and none are going to be in any sense capable of providing the

smooth perfection that either of us would like to ascribe
to our own systems.

Throughout my own effort I indicated step-by-step
that I am supporting the existing system, an admittedly
imperfect system, one whose imperfections are clear for
all to see because it is meeting the test of practical and
continuous current application and subject to the constraints and the premises of the kind I have just mentioned and with which we are bound to live. Whatever
any of us would like to do about recreating the image
of mankind for the sake of providing a simpler setting
for our own formulation of economic arrangements, we
don't really have that choice.

As a matter of fact, I would like to turn in the other
direction and ask him a number of questions that were
raised by his paper, in the hope that as we work these
over back and forth we may be able to get a little
closer, at least, to a clearer understanding of our differences. But I hope we can see them as they become important in the real world, and not this time through a
fanciful creation of his imagination.

I really wonder, first of all, Milton, why you used
the description you did throughout your paper of the
patterns of central bank action that occur in foreign
exchange markets. I am sure you know that operations
in foreign exchange markets have never been conducted
in that way. I realize that economists don't have to know
all of the mechanics of every process with which they
are dealing. We can generalize about big issues in the

same way that we can drive a car without having to know how the motor works. But we do have to know, and be able to tell others, which end to put in water and which end to put in fuel.

Yet the whole analysis of the way in which foreign exchange markets function as set forth throughout your paper, Milton, is simply completely out of context with the way in which these markets do operate. To have a starting point, we ought to begin at least with recognition of the fact that foreign exchange rates are maintained by the various central banks of the world by trading in their own currency against dollars. Each maintains its own upper and its own lower limit. Each, within those limits, most of the time maintains a rate which is close to parity and never even reaches either outer limit. The central banks are operating under the discipline of a set of guidelines which they realize, in self-defense, they must respect. Otherwise, the whole system, if there weren't these guidelines, would break down into a sequence of competitive depreciations which would create the conditions of bilateralism. There would be an insulation of the frontiers of each country from the trading potentials of others. That seems to me inherent in the nature of an unstable exchange-rate system. (By the way, if I were, in my language, to transcribe the terminology that describes this debate, it would not be the romantically appealing "free versus fixed" exchange rates. Quite the contrary, what we are talking about is "unstable" as opposed to "stable" exchange rates and the conditions which either of these make possible for the maintenance and expansion of trade and capital movements in the world.)

Now, my second question is: Why is it that he assumes at one part of his analysis that there can be complete elasticity in domestic supply and demand to make adjustment to rate changes instantaneous within an economy? Then elsewhere he assumes that a rate change will, in fact, completely insulate the economy as it exists from the need for any internal change?

In *Newsweek* one week ago, Professor Friedman wrote that the way in which to solve the whole balance-of-payments problem is just to let the rate move, nothing else will have to happen. That would, he said, free the authorities within every country to maintain whatever domestic policy they wish to pursue.

What sort of an adjustment process is this, other than an assumption that the rate would so change as to preserve at all times the status quo?

And if that is the way the rate is going to function, what it really means is the building of a wall around every country; this is going to prevent those healthful corrective adjustments that he has already identified in beginning the discussion tonight.

And then, a third question. Why does he say at one point in the discussion that rate fluctuations alone can remove adjustment problems, then at another point claim that the ideal result, the world we want to have, is one in which, although rates might be free to move, they are in fact stable? How can he have it in this respect both ways?

Or a fourth question. If stable rates are the ideal, what is introduced by having the potential for flexibility? What do you get except more uncertainty, especially among those countries in a real world which will in each successive episode of internal domestic difficulty find a way, if they aren't limited by guidelines of norms and behavior, to depreciate their rates, one after another, to gain a momentary trade advantage? Ours is a world of red-blooded competition. In that kind of world, the existence of a fluctuating rate system is inevitably going to mean a wider band of uncertainty, with all the complications from it that I have already mentioned.

And then from this how can he go on to say that he is going to bury decently the view that speculation under floating rates can be destabilizing? He says actually there has never been a study that showed this destabilizing effect. Now I don't pretend to read all that I should, but the Aliber work in the *Yale Economic Essays*, about five years ago certainly shows that in the case of all the European countries after World War I, that is, all those which Aliber analyzed, under the conditions then prevailing, the effect of fluctuating rates was to create a speculative aggravation, a sequence of destabilizing influences.

And then my fifth question. Why did he leave out of his paper, and also leave out of what he has just been saying, all analysis of capital movements? Any part of his exposition, if it holds at all, can be turned upside down if there were to be the kind of capital movement which would weaken or strengthen an exchange rate and in turn create opportunities for exporters or importers in a given country. This would lead, in turn, just because the capital movement had occurred, to a decisive change in the attractiveness within a given country of one kind of export, one kind of production, one kind of import or another.

How can you say, if the rate is free to move and if you expect it to move, that you are going to keep the domestic economy completely insulated and free to follow its own program regardless of what goes on outside? Particularly if you take into account the fact that trade and capital movements both have to be reconciled in the given exchange-rate system. There has to be a compromise. There's no perfect solution.

The nearest approximation or series of successive approximations we have been able to devise is that countries will pursue domestic policies under the armed truce that prevails with a fixed-rate system. We can't deny them the right to pursue domestic policies. They are just determined to do it, whether we legislate it in or out. They will pursue domestic policies that in their own way are bound to be affected by the reactions from any change in exchange rates produced either by capital movements or the resulting changes in trade flow.

Another question, my sixth, getting back to the discipline that he talked about. How can he assert that, as concerns the system I've been trying to defend, all adjustment under this system occurs only with controls? Certainly there have been a lot of controls. This system is imperfect. At the present stage it is certainly doing much less well than at many other times in the past. But a good many effective adjustments have been accomplished too.

What is going to change the nature of American readiness to take the kinds of steps necessary to accomplish an effective adjustment if the exchange rate is free, as against the present discipline of a fixed-rate system? To be sure, the discipline has led us into some strange and wonderful things, but it has also persistently been a dominating influence in guiding us toward the same decisions that we should seek for domestic reasons, the same emphasis. We fail, as human beings do, to do the perfect job, but the same emphasis remains on the need for price stability, for productivity improvement, and so on.

The present system is geared to the assumption that there will be imperfections all the way around. But we will use reserves to provide time for correction. We won't have to have the sort of instantaneous shake of a system from one side to the other, as a rate change occurs, with one industry flooded with demand one day and drought the next, because capital movements have turned the exchanges and altered the exchange rate.

Finally, my seventh question, and this only repeats

a point that I have woven through many of these other questions, how can he under a system of flexible rates, if he wants to live in a real world, avoid the risk, the exposure to competitive exchange depreciation, the related reinforcing of potential inflationary developments, and the serious risk of misallocation of capital around the world?

PROFESSOR G. WARREN NUTTER, University of Virginia, coordinator of the Rational Debate: It is the desire of both participants to have a free exchange insofar as we have time left within our first hour, so I am going to bow to this and allow the debaters to talk to each other for the next 15 minutes.

PROFESSOR FRIEDMAN: Let me take up first the problem of competitive depreciation. This is really a false issue. I don't know what color herring but it's a herring.

The experience to which Dr. Roosa refers is the experience of the 1930s. Now, we need to have historical perspective. First of all, it's important to know that the 1930s were a product of fixed rates, not of floating rates. The United States and the other countries of the world had a fixed rate in 1929. When the United States embarked on deflation and proceeded to reduce its money stock, the rest of the world was forced into a major catastrophe. So the origin of that move was fixed rates, not flexible rates.

It was only when countries got off the fixed rates that improvements were made. When Britain went off gold in 1931, she was able to break the link with our contraction.

It is worth noting that the countries that stayed on the fixed-rate system were the ones that saw the depression come to an end latest, the United States in 1933, France in 1934, and so on. On the other side, the countries that broke the link with fixed rates and went on to floating or flexible rates were the ones that got out of the depression first.

In the second place, a system under which you have adjustable pegs is a very different system from a system under which you have floating rates.

In the third place, the 1930s saw widespread unemployment in many countries. Countries were seeking to control their exchange rates by governmental means and to depreciate against one another. In the present situation you have relatively full employment, and I trust you will continue to. What does a country have to do to depreciate competitively against the U.S. dollar? It has to provide us with interest-free loans.

We are utter fools if we don't say to any country in the world, if you want to depreciate competitively, fine and dandy. What that means is that you are prepared to sell us your goods at a lower price than that at which we could otherwise buy them. There's nothing wrong with that. There is no mileage to be gained from competitive depreciation by anybody in a world of reasonably full employment.

This is, again, I think, something that Dr. Roosa has dreamed up to scare children with.

But let me go to the more important analytical issue that Bob raises. Throughout his discussion, he confuses different kinds of adjustments. I ask him what his adjustment mechanism is and he says to me, "Well, how can you say that under a floating rate you have instantaneous adjustment? Aren't you going to have a country with goods flooding in one day and flooding out the next day? Aren't capital movements going to cause all of the farmers of the country to plant twice as many acres this month and next month to go out and dig them up?"

The answer is, I believe, that you must distinguish three kinds of adjustments which are quite different: adjustments to monetary disturbances; adjustments in the international sector itself; adjustments in the rest of the economy.

In the first place, there are those cases in which external disturbances represent monetary changes abroad or at home, in which there is no need for "real" adjustments, for adjustments in the flows of goods and services. If a foreign country, to take an extreme case, doubles its price level, then a halving of the exchange rate means that no adjustment is required by either country because relative prices are left unchanged.

In such a case, rate fluctuations can remove adjustment problems because they make it unnecessary to make real adjustments in response to monetary disturbances.

The simplest example in modern times is Germany.
Germany in the past ten years had to make real adjustments. She had to export capital she didn't intend
to export. She had to change interest rates internally
she otherwise wouldn't have had to change because, with
a fixed-rate system, Germany was being affected by the
monetary inflation in the rest of the world.

Point number one therefore is: Insofar as exchange-
rate adjustments offset monetary disturbances in different countries, the exchange-rate movements eliminate
the necessity for making physical adjustments. In those
cases they do make adjustment painless.

Second, there are external disturbances which reflect changes in real conditions of trade—the fact that
some country has developed a new way of producing
automobiles which makes them more competitive with
respect to us; or that there is an increase in the world
demand for copper. These real changes do require real
adjustment in an economy.

But they require it only in certain sectors. They require it in the sectors which are affected by these changes.

Under a fixed-rate system the problem is that, if such
a change occurs, it requires the adjustment in one sector to be made by an adjustment in the rest of the
economy. To illustrate, let us suppose that in the U.S.
there is, suddenly, a great increase in the demand for
copper. Under a fixed-rate system, this disturbs our
balance of payments. We tend to have a deficit. To
adjust to this, we would have to lower our whole price

level just to permit a rise in the relative price of copper.

Under a floating-rate system, the exchange rate makes that part of the adjustment which would otherwise have to be made by the economy as a whole and the relative prices of the particular commodities that are involved make that part of the adjustment which corresponds to a real adjustment.

The virtue of a floating-exchange-rate system is not that it eliminates the need for all adjustments. The virtue is rather that it minimizes the problem of adjustment because it makes it unnecessary to make real adjustments to monetary changes and to change relative prices through changing the total price level. Of the three types of adjustments I listed initially, it eliminates the necessity for two.

Now, I may say that covers quite a number of Bob's comments. I think most of his comments and half of his questions derive from not distinguishing among these three kinds of adjustments.

With respect to capital movements, I don't intend to leave out capital movements at all. We want a world in which you have free capital movements. We want to welcome and encourage capital movements. Capital movements do require real adjustments. Dr. Roosa sometimes talks as if under a fixed-rate system you could have a capital movement without an adjustment. That isn't so.

If Canada is going to import capital, in the real sense, then there has to be a difference between its exports and its imports.

If the U.S. is going to export capital, there has to be an excess of exports over imports to finance it.

Of course, capital movements have to affect the real balance of payments. The question is: What is the mechanism of adjustment?

Under a fixed-rate system the mechanism of adjustment must be differential price movements. The country that seeks to export capital must have its prices decline relative to countries that want to import capital.

Under a floating-rate system the adjustments can take place much more easily because the exchange rate will then move and this will tend to create the balance-of-trade difference required to accommodate the capital movement.

Let me just make one more comment—about Dr. Roosa's differentiation between my description of exchange markets and the way they really work. He says that as a day-to-day matter foreign exchange rates are maintained by central banks with upper and lower limits, that my description of foreign banks having a requirement to maintain an upper limit and the U.S. having the requirement to maintain a lower limit is not valid. In an operational way, of course, he's right. He knows much more about the day-to-day operations than I do. But on the basic level of principle I do not believe that my description is invalid.

The point is that foreign countries are willing to sell and buy within these ranges and do what I described as our job because we have been willing to trade their extra dollars for gold. At that point, they are, in effect, acting as our agents and it has been our willingness to provide them with gold when they felt they had acquired too many dollars that has made them willing to appear to act in the market to support our rate at the bottom. That really is the mechanics of the way we have operated our side of the deal.

DR. ROOSA: Thanks, Milton. I do think that it is important to repeat again that our aims, as they persist through all of this, are clearly the same. Despite the variations that are introduced for the purpose of making one point or another, we both see that the world is going to function more effectively on an exchange-rate system which provides, most of the time, stable relations among countries so that there is a basis for measuring what the impact is of a change within any country.

In technology, we both hope to produce a result indicating whether or not the automobile now producible at cheaper prices in the United States is going to be exported or not.

If, whenever there were a technological improvement on the part of this or any other country, all that happened was that exchange rates instantly moved against the country then in a position to move into another foreign market, what would have been accomplished, of course, through a flexible-rate system would be the kind of isolation that would prevent —

PROFESSOR FRIEDMAN: No, Bob. No, no, Bob.

What would move the rate? Only that they were selling the goods.

DR. ROOSA: Well, if they find that they have a competitive advantage and if the surplus that they are acquiring is not providing them with a stronger rate, then their competitive advantage would go on providing a continued opportunity for them to export for a while. If, finally, the rate moves, the net result of their having a stronger rate is—

PROFESSOR FRIEDMAN: No, no, no, no.

DR. ROOSA: —for them eventually to import. Well, all right.

PROFESSOR FRIEDMAN: Your mechanics are wrong.

DR. ROOSA: Let me skip over that one and we'll come back, because I shouldn't have digressed too far into this one because this is only the starter and I do want to also get back to your point about the nightmare of competitive depreciation, to which this leads and we can come back to the technical point about the productivity change in a minute.

First of all, the study I referred to covered the 1920s, after World War I, and not the 1930s, although I did, in other connections, refer to the 1930s as well. Anything is going to be a result of the system that has been prevailing so we can't say that just because flexible rates during their period didn't work that only shows that fixed rates are a failure. The net result is that after flexible rates were allowed to function for a while, were supposed to be taking over, every country in its own wisdom and judgment returned to a fixed-rate system because they needed the protection against mutual combativeness that is embodied in the drive produced for competitive exchange-rate depreciation.

So I can't agree, Milton, that this is something to be dismissed only as my private nightmare. I have a lot of them. But not this one.

And on another point—I know that this isn't exactly what you mean, but it is an illusion for you to say that the end result of all this is a satisfactory solution because we just get a lot of interest-free loans from other countries. They obviously aren't interest-free in any case. Foreigners do hold interest-earning money market assets here. But what does actually produce the difference leads me into my comment on capital movements. It is not merely that we were prepared to pay out gold. It is the fact that the dollar is the transactions currency, the balance-holding currency and, indeed, the interest-earning currency which provides another part of this total system.

What is part of the real world in which we live today and is a byproduct of this interest-earning dollar is that we also have a Euro-dollar market of a $15 billion dimension. In this Euro-dollar market there can be changes that will, under a free-rate system, affect the exchange rate of the dollar without making one iota of difference in the movement of goods in or out of the United States in relation to those transactions. Now, this is a fact of life. This is no one's creation of imagination, Milton, and we have to live with some of the conditions of the world as they have evolved.

If we were to inject a free-rate system amid this existing set of arrangements, arrangements that have evolved out of the convenience, necessity, and requirements of responses to free impulses, if not fully free markets, we would find that shifts in this kind of capital movement would be producing changes in the exchange rate for the dollar that would have repercussions on the whole economy. These repercussions you can't escape if the terms of trade for American products are changed by movement into or out of Euro-dollars on the part of the holders of other currencies.

Now, to get to your point on adjustments, Milton. I have to confess, I don't know whether I was daydreaming or what went wrong, but I only heard two of the three kinds you promised to describe. I do think what you have said is important and it has been a real contribution to get the clarification of these distinctions, because I agree that it does make a difference as to which of these we are talking about.

If, in the first case, we talk about differences that originate from monetary changes at home or abroad, and if in those circumstances you rely upon a rate change to neutralize whatever the superficial influences in the monetary system are inserting into an otherwise balanced relationship, then that conceptually is possible. Certainly it is conceptually possible. But this does mean that in order to take care of every change of any significance in the monetary performance of any other country, the exchange rate for the world against the United States is going to have to change.

Now, Milton, you can't have it both ways. You can't say that you want to live in a world of stable rates and get the advantage of it and, at the same time, say that as a part of the adjustment process that the United States must, in this way, be subjected to the influence of wrong or right monetary policies on the part of every other country in the world. You have to choose.

Under the present system we have those hard choices to make. I am not trying to say that we can escape them. I am saying that these are a part of the inherent issues that have to be worked through under either system and you just can't escape them by a flip definition.

In the same way, when there are real changes in the conditions of trade, we get down to the problem that you and I were trying to talk about a minute ago. We don't want to run too far beyond our time limit here but I think we could come back to that for a minute.

Suppose that the exchange rate of the United States is improved because, everything else having remained the same, there has been an improvement in our exports because we produce something more cheaply and those goods move abroad. Starting here, the first effect should be an increase, a strengthening of our own exchange rate. We are earning more.

PROFESSOR FRIEDMAN: Because we are selling more.

DR. ROOSA: Because we are selling more. And now —

PROFESSOR FRIEDMAN: We're buying more.

DR. ROOSA: Yes. Now, what happens —

PROFESSOR FRIEDMAN: You're buying more.

DR. ROOSA: What I want to know, because this is where we get the answer, is: are you saying that the minute that this rise of exports happens we, in fact, get an instantaneous adjustment in rate and thereby get an instantaneous adjustment in terms of importing an equal additional amount?

PROFESSOR FRIEDMAN: By selling more, the exporters acquire additional foreign exchange. Who provides it to them?

DR. ROOSA: The person who buys the exports, whoever he is.

PROFESSOR FRIEDMAN: All right. Now what do the exporters do with the additional foreign exchange?

If you've got a market that has to clear and there is no central bank for filling in this gap, they sell the foreign exchange to people who want to use it to buy foreign goods. That is what makes our exchange rate strengthen—that is, makes the price of the dollar in terms of foreign exchange go up.

DR. ROOSA: Oh, now, that's another assumption. That's really important to track back. You are now saying that this version of the flexible-rate system is one in which central banks do nothing.

PROFESSOR FRIEDMAN: They do something, they follow their internal policy. They do not intervene in the foreign exchange market.

DR. ROOSA: All right. Then we just have an absolute dichotomy because my premise is that you can't keep them out.

PROFESSOR FRIEDMAN: Just for the moment, assume that they are out and that they're not at liberty themselves to take any action affecting the rate itself.

DR. ROOSA: Yes.

PROFESSOR FRIEDMAN: Now, we sell abroad, and we sell for foreign exchange. What do the sellers do with the foreign exchange they get? Do they hold it? If they hold it, the rate won't change.

DR. ROOSA: Of course, it's possible that this will then take the form of this kind of capital movement. Capital has moved and it is undergirded with a movement of exports.

PROFESSOR FRIEDMAN: It could be that the people who sell the additional goods abroad finance it by making a loan essentially to the foreign country to buy it.

DR. ROOSA: Yes, that is one possibility.

PROFESSOR FRIEDMAN: Then you are in identically the same position as the position you approve of under a fixed rate.

DR. ROOSA: Yes, quite.

PROFESSOR FRIEDMAN: And the rate won't change.

DR. ROOSA: And the rate doesn't change, that is right.

PROFESSOR FRIEDMAN: That won't happen.

DR. ROOSA: Why?

PROFESSOR FRIEDMAN: If these people didn't want to make a loan before, why should they want to make a loan now? What happens is that the people who now acquire the extra foreign exchange try to sell it for dollars. How can they sell it for dollars? Only by offering more foreign exchange per dollar—

DR. ROOSA: Yes.

PROFESSOR FRIEDMAN: —and why do other people then want to buy the foreign exchange?

DR. ROOSA: Yes.

PROFESSOR FRIEDMAN: Because if they can get more foreign exchange for a dollar, this makes foreign goods cheaper to them. So they buy the foreign exchange to spend it on foreign goods, which means that our imports go up. So that the exchange rate has the effect of adding to exports and adding to imports, except for transitional capital movements.

DR. ROOSA: All right. Now, you see this is again an illustration of what I mean when I say you can't have it both ways. I'll take that version because that could be one version.

PROFESSOR FRIEDMAN: All right.

DR. ROOSA: You can't at the same time say that,

this having occurred, that we are able with a flexible rate to insulate the American economy from the impact of a change.

PROFESSOR FRIEDMAN: We don't insulate the American economy from the change in our real competitiveness in exports or our increased imports. What we do is to insulate the American economy from any secondary effect of monetary changes abroad; and we make this adjustment to the change in real factors without requiring all prices in the United States to go up and down.

DR. ROOSA: Yes, I thought that's what I was saying.

PROFESSOR FRIEDMAN: I quite agree with you that it is wrong to say that we insulate the American economy from everything. We insulate it from those external events that do not require changes in the pattern of production and consumption. We do have to adjust to external events that do require changes in the pattern of production and consumption. It is desirable that we should.

DR. ROOSA: Yes.

PROFESSOR FRIEDMAN: You and I both want us to adjust to those.

DR. ROOSA: That's right, that's right. I have no problem with that.

PROFESSOR FRIEDMAN: And it is precisely because we eliminate the unnecessary adjustments that we can have a larger tolerance for those adjustments that both you and I want us to make.

DR. ROOSA: The other condition is that at the same time that this isolated sequence is occurring that the same freedom of rates which has been operating here in this delightful way is not also being subjected to other kinds of influences. For example, in the area of short-term capital movements.

PROFESSOR FRIEDMAN: Take the case of short-term capital movements. With fixed rates, you undoubtedly have destabilizing movements of short-term capital because whenever there is a possibility that the rate will be devalued, people have nothing to lose by getting out of the currency. If they are wrong, they can go back in.

But consider the case of floating rates in the Euro-dollar market. How can people get out of dollars? Only by persuading somebody else to buy the dollars. In order to persuade somebody else, they have to offer dollars at a lower price.

DR. ROOSA: Sure.

PROFESSOR FRIEDMAN: They pay something for the capital movement. Actual and potential exchange-rate fluctuations inhibit capital movement, so that with flexible rates, you are far less likely to have volatile capital movements than with fixed rates.

I have looked at Aliber's study and, as you know, there are also a series of studies that have appeared in International Monetary Papers by Tsiang on postwar European experience.

And in addition, there have been a series of studies on South American countries, and more recently the Cana-

THE BALANCE OF PAYMENTS

dian experience. All of these suggested the absence of destabilizing capital movements, but this isn't the place where we can thrash it out.

DR. ROOSA: No, to be sure. But all I was saying on this one was that there is evidence both ways, not only one way. Your original statement was that you were going to bury the thing because no one else had any contrary experience.

PROFESSOR FRIEDMAN: As I interpret Aliber's study — well, again, I don't think we ought to be going into that. Maybe we can put it into the record.
[Note subsequently added by Professor Friedman:

The study referred to is Robert Z. Aliber, "Speculation in the Foreign Exchanges: The European Experience, 1919-1926," *Yale Economics Essays*, Spring, 1962, pp. 171-245.

Aliber studied experience in five countries: Britain, France, Belgium, the Netherlands, and Switzerland. On the issue under discussion, he concludes that speculation was destabilizing in France in the sense that speculatively induced changes in exchange rates produced cost-push inflation internally, which was subsequently validated by governmental policy. Thus while speculators were *ex post* proved correct—hence in one sense stabilizing—he argues that they themselves produced the internal price movements that proved them correct. This is certainly a possibility and perhaps it is correct, but I find Aliber's evidence far from convincing. It consists mainly of the inability to find evidence supporting one alternative interpretation of the inflation, namely, that it reflected government deficits, rather than of affirmative evidence of the influence of speculatively produced changes in exchange rates on internal policy.

For Belgium, Aliber also finds evidence of destabilizing speculation, arising, he argues, from "the strong speculative belief that the Belgium franc and the French franc should exchange on a one-for-one basis."

For Britain, he concludes that there was no destabilizing speculation but that "speculators forced the United Kingdom authorities to honor their commitment to return to the gold standard at the prewar parity when this was not the path of economic wisdom."

For Netherlands and Switzerland, he also finds that speculation was not destabilizing but argues that "both countries . . . easily could have become subject to a speculative attack which proved self-justifying."

At bottom, therefore, Aliber's negative conclusions about flexible rates rest primarily on the experience of France, and even for France, on a possible but not demonstrated link between speculation and internal policy.]

DISCUSSION

FIRST SESSION

LOUIS DOMBROWSKI, *Chicago Tribune:* Professor Friedman, what effect would a serious economic crisis in the United States have on floating exchange rates throughout the world?

PROFESSOR FRIEDMAN: You mean a serious internal crsis?

MR. DOMBROWSKI: Yes.

PROFESSOR FRIEDMAN: If you had a worldwide system of floating exchange rates and the U.S. had a serious internal crisis, the effect would largely be restricted to the United States.

In most circumstances, the effect would be that the dollar would appreciate in terms of other currencies. Because if the U.S. had a serious economic crsis, it would have unemployment and declining prices. Therefore American goods would tend to become cheap relative to world goods. This would, in the first instance, make for a balance-of-payments surplus, which would be offset by an appreciation of the exchange rate.

The situation would be very different from what happened from 1929 to 1931. At that time we had rigid exchange rates, so the U.S. crisis pulled down the rest of the world. The key reason why there was a world-wide economic crisis from 1929 to 1931 was because the United States deflated and because most of the world was on a real gold standard linked to the United States.

Evidence that that was the case for 1929 to 1931 turns out to be readily available in the case of China. China was on a silver standard when the rest of the world was on a gold standard. As a result China had the equivalent of floating exchange rates, because the price of silver in terms of gold could change. China did not feel the worldwide depression from 1929 to 1931. The total exports of China stayed up, income within China stayed up. China was affected by the world depression for the first time in September, 1931, when Britain went off gold, and the pound sterling depreciated relative to the Chinese currency.

That's a very dramatic example of the effectiveness of a floating exchange rate in insulating a country from disturbances within other countries.

Obviously, I don't mean to say that other countries wouldn't be affected at all. If the United States had a great depression, our demand for their goods would go down, there would be a decline in real demand. This would produce adverse effects on other countries. But these adverse effects would not be compounded by our forcing monetary deflation on them.

They might have some decline in exports, but they would not be required in addition to adjust their whole price level, which is what we forced the rest of the world to do in 1929.

HARVEY SEGAL, *Washington Post:* Professor Friedman, two questions. First, are you surprised at the durability of this adjustable peg system that was set up after Bretton Woods? And the second question: Can we get a change in the present system of movement, let's say toward flexible exchange rates, without having a crisis as a practical matter?

PROFESSOR FRIEDMAN: On the first one, the durability of the adjustable peg system, one has to ask what you mean by being durable. Let's look at the period since Bretton Woods. There have been quite a substantial number of major adjustments. Britain devalued sharply, twice I guess it was, wasn't it? Germany appreciated once.

You had a switch from a dollar shortage, when most of the European countries had extensive exchange controls, import quotas, restrictions on trade to a dollar surplus, which meant that restrictions on trade were reduced in Europe and increased in the United States.

So I'm not sure it has really been so terribly durable. And, of course, if you go outside the range of the European countries, why then, in the rest of the world it clearly has not been. But I grant you that the major issue is about Europe and the U.S. and not the rest of the world.

Now, your second question. As a practical matter can you get a change away from the present system?

As a practical political matter, I think there are only two sets of circumstances under which you are likely to get floating rates. One is if you have a major crisis. The second is if you have an effective change in government from one party to another, and the floating rates are established within the first two weeks. Let me illustrate the second possibility with a concrete case. Harold Wilson made a terrible mistake. Suppose within the first week of his coming to office the first time, not the second time, he had gone on the BBC (British Broadcasting Corporation) and had said, "On coming into office and examining the figures on the balance of payments and our foreign balance position, I was shocked at the state in which I found them. I hadn't realized that the Conservative Government had done such a terrible job and left us in such an awful position. Under these circumstances I can see only two things to do. Either we can go in for a severe austerity program, for extensive controls and tightening of the belt in order to redeem the mistakes of our predecessors, or else we can devalue. I don't know quite where to devalue to, so we ought to float for a while until we find out. I have chosen to cut the Gordian Knot and get us out from under the mess we were left in by floating."

If Wilson had done that, in my opinion he would have done for the Labor Party by that one act what Erhard did in 1948 for the Christian Democratic Party in Germany. Erhard's one act on that Sunday in 1948 put the Christian Democratic Party in power for over

20 years. And I believe that if Wilson had had the foresight to do what I have just suggested, and if he had accompanied floating the exchange rate with the elimination of other restrictions, you might have had the same kind of economic miracle in Britain that you had in Germany after 1948.

But once two weeks or so had passed, it was too late, because by then Wilson had said, "We shall defend the pound, we shall not devalue." He was committed and it's very difficult to back out of a commitment.

President Kennedy could have done it in the United States within his first two weeks. President Johnson could not do it because he was the same party. If the Conservatives come into power in Britain, they could do it in Britain. If the Republicans come into power in the United States, they could do it in the United States. Speaking politically and realistically, it seems to me that those are the only possible circumstances: a crisis, or during the first two weeks of a new government of a new party.

What are the chances? With respect to a crisis, anybody who tries to predict the occurrence of a crisis is, I think, very foolish. You are sitting on a powder keg, but if nobody lights the fuse, nobody will know you're sitting on a powder keg. A major international crisis is the kind of thing that happens every 20 or 30 years. The odds against it happening in any particular six-months period are very great.

Therefore I would not want to predict that at any

immediately foreseeable date you are going to have a crisis. Yet I don't want to rule out the possibility that one of these days you may very well have an international crisis which blows up to such dimensions that the only way you can get out of it is by letting the exchange rates go.

HOWARD S. PIQUET, Library of Congress: Professor Friedman, I have admired always the manner in which you have testified before the committees. I think that you have not been too effective in getting anything done.

PROFESSOR FRIEDMAN: I hate to have you denigrate the role of truth in that way.

DR. PIQUET: I'm coming to the question. You have pretty much taken for granted that adoption of a floating exchange rate such as in answer to your last question would also be accompanied by a change of heart on the part of ourselves and other countries with respect to trade controls, quotas, and so on.

If we were to adopt the one without the other, that is, the floating exchange rate without a real determined movement toward giving up the idea of quotas, wouldn't we have the danger of simply doing what we did between the two world wars, of having competitive exchange bargaining—not bargaining, but—

PROFESSOR FRIEDMAN: Depreciation?

DR. PIQUET: —exchange warfare—

PROFESSOR FRIEDMAN: No.

DR. PIQUET: —exchange depreciation.

PROFESSOR FRIEDMAN: No. No, we would not. Let me separate my answer to that.

Even if we didn't give up any quotas, it would be better to have floating exchange rates than what we now have, because what we now have keeps forcing more and more quotas, more and more restrictions, on us. Moreover, if we once had floating rates, I think it would be very much more difficult to maintain the system of quotas and restrictions.

Maybe I am wrong, maybe we would maintain them. However, the fear of exchange depreciation is a particular example of confusing a system of adjustable pegs with a floating rate.

The competitive exchange depreciation that we had during the 1930s was competitive depreciation with adjustable pegs, not with a floating rate.

DR. PIQUET: That was gold.

PROFESSOR FRIEDMAN: What's that?

DR. PIQUET: That was gold still, in some cases.

PROFESSOR FRIEDMAN: Well, yes. But it involved changing the price of gold.

DR. PIQUET: That's right.

PROFESSOR FRIEDMAN: It involved an adjustable peg, moving the exchange rate from one level to another. There is another and even more fundamental difference between the situation in the thirties, and what the situation would be now with floating rates. In the thirties you had worldwide unemployment. Countries were anxious to give goods away if it provided employment at home. And other countries, foolishly enough, were not willing to take goods for nothing if it created unemployment.

At the moment we are not in that situation, and we're not likely to be. If other countries want to engage in competitive exchange depreciation, we are crazy if we don't welcome it. What are they doing when they competitively depreciate? They are saying to us "Look, if you'll take some of our goods for cheap, we'll give them to you." Well, let's not be fools, let's take it.

So I think the answer to your question is that in a world where you have reasonably full employment, something like a reasonably operating system, there is no incentive to countries to engage in competitive depreciation, and there is no incentive for other countries to try to avoid it.

DR. PIQUET: Would you be equally as firm in saying there would be no incentive to impose import quotas?

PROFESSOR FRIEDMAN: There surely would be no incentive to impose import quotas.

DR. PIQUET: Why not?

PROFESSOR FRIEDMAN: Why should we impose import quotas?

DR. PIQUET: I don't say we. They.

PROFESSOR FRIEDMAN: Why should they? Why should they impose import quotas? They can't—under floating exchange rates they can only import more from us if they export more to us.

DR. PIQUET: The logic is impeccable. That I understand.

PROFESSOR FRIEDMAN: Well.

DR. PIQUET: But I'm talking about the political reality of how politicians react.

PROFESSOR FRIEDMAN: Right. But how would politicians react under those circumstances? Why would they have an incentive to impose import quotas that they otherwise would not impose? As we all know, the forces of protection are always very strong. Particular industries have special vested interests. They are always going to try to get governmental measures that they expect to operate in their favor.

The argument I am making is that the existence of rigid rates pegged by government strengthens the special interests who are trying to get measures in their favor. Maybe they would succeed anyway, but their road would be a little harder with floating rates.

DR. PIQUET: I follow your logic completely. How do I tell Senator Dirksen though?

PROFESSOR FRIEDMAN: I'm not sure I know what it is that you have difficulty telling Senator Dirksen. What is it that you can't tell him?

DR. PIQUET: Well, I'm giving him simply as án example.

PROFESSOR FRIEDMAN: I know. Oh, I understand that. The thing you tell him is very simple. You tell him that the floating rate provides general protection for all export industries at one fell swoop and you don't have to have it for one industry after another separately. The point I've tried to emphasize is that under a fixed rate, the argument against protection is subtle, sophisticated, and difficult to get across. Under a floating rate it is simplicity itself.

What are you afraid of? Are you afraid that we are going to import a lot from abroad? We can't. The attempt to do so would drive the price of foreign currencies up which will stimulate our exports.

The movable exchange rate provides automatic protection. You therefore can dispense with this wasteful, silly system of protecting industry A separately and B separately and C separately. Let's do it in one fell swoop. And it seems to me that is the argument you make.

DR. PIQUET: I'll change jobs with you.

PROFESSOR FRIEDMAN: At what price?

HERBERT BRATTER, *Banking* magazine: If I understand you correctly, these floating rates would soon result in a congregation of countries attached to the dollar and perhaps other countries attached to the pound and others to the yen and so on. So in effect you would have floating rates not between a mass of individual currencies, but between a few blocs of currencies. Is that right?

PROFESSOR FRIEDMAN: As a practical matter that is probably the way it would work. You would have also many separate individual countries, probably Brazil, Argentina, Chile, Colombia, countries like that, which would not attach themselves. They might, but very likely they would not attach themselves.

MR. BRATTER: Well, wouldn't the countries attaching themselves to the dollar be opting for fixed rates rather than floating rates by that very action?

PROFESSOR FRIEDMAN: They would be opting for fixed rates. And it is not necessarily wrong for them to do so.

Don't misunderstand me. I'm not saying that there never is a case for fixed rates. I'm saying there is never a case for pegged rates, which is quite a different thing.

The point is that it makes a great deal of sense for these other countries to tie themselves to the dollar in the sense of unifying their currency with the dollar—provided we adopt a reasonably stable internal policy. Of course if we are foolish and stupid, if we let ourselves in for another crisis such as was suggested before, well then, they would be very smart to break the tie with the dollar.

But so long as we maintain a reasonably stable internal policy, it makes a great deal of sense for smaller countries for whom foreign trade is a large part of their total trade to tie themselves to the dollar.

MR. BRATTER: How would those smaller countries which are working for or asking for commodity agreements to peg the price of coffee or cocoa or something else fare under such a system?

PROFESSOR FRIEDMAN: The commodity stabilization programs, that is a different question. That's a question—

MR. BRATTER: They want fixed prices.

PROFESSOR FRIEDMAN: What's that?

MR. BRATTER: Those who want stabilization want fixed prices, fixed relationships.

PROFESSOR FRIEDMAN: Yes. I think that the United States makes an enormous mistake by participating in any such stabilization agreements. They are cartel agreements that we ought to oppose. We ought to be in favor of free market prices for commodities as well as free markets for currencies. If those countries still want to engage in those stabilization agreements, we ought not to support them or cooperate with them.

MR. BRATTER: Why did Canada abandon floating rates after 12 years?

PROFESSOR FRIEDMAN: That is a very good question, and I'll be glad to indicate why. The first point that has to be made is that floating rates are not a guarantee of sensible internal monetary policy. You can have silly internal monetary policy with fixed rates, you can have silly internal monetary policy with floating rates. All floating rates do is to make it possible for you to have a sensible internal monetary policy without considering the rest of the world.

What happened in Canada? It's a very interesting and instructive story, because the reason—I'll come to the end first and then I'll go back and trace it out. The reason Canada went off floating rates was because they were working so well, and their internal monetary policy was so bad. Let me illustrate that a little bit. From 1950 to 1952 the Bank of Canada was interfering in the market for the Canadian dollar. You had a truly floating rate from about 1952 on.

From 1952 to 1962, so far as exchange rates were concerned, they worked very well. The rate floated, but it didn't move around a great deal. Speculation was clearly stabilizing. Short-term movements were mild. The Bank of Canada largely stayed out of it.

But side by side with that, the Canadian internal monetary policy was a very bad monetary policy. It was an extremely erratic monetary policy, particularly when J. E. Coyne was Governor of the Bank of Canada. He tried to lengthen the maturity distribution of the Canadian debt, and did it in a very clumsy way. In general, he followed an erratic and generally disturbing monetary policy that left Canada with relatively high levels of unemployment.

He also, as you know, was very much in favor of Canadianization of industry, opposed to the import of capital from the United States. So he was in favor of trying to interfere with the free flow of capital from the United States. That was one of the reasons why he followed the kinds of monetary policy he did.

When Coyne finally left, there was an attempt to do something effective about the unemployment problem in Canada. But instead of correcting their bad monetary policy internally, which would have been a sensible thing to do, they said, "Ah, here is a floating rate. We will force the rate down and stimulate employment inside Canada by discouraging imports and encouraging exports. We will try to engage in the kind of thing Mr. Piquet was talking about, competitive currency devaluation."

And so what happened? The Bank of Canada announced that it was going to try to force the price of the Canadian dollar down by exchange speculation. The speculators didn't believe it. The Bank of Canada speculated against the Canadian dollar, and the speculators absorbed the funds, and nothing happened. The Canadian rates stayed fairly fixed. So the Bank of Canada, said, "We haven't been doing this on a big enough scale; we're going to do it yet." Then the Bank made bigger and bigger announcements and engaged in larger and larger speculative actions.

Finally it started the rate moving down. Once the rate started moving down, the speculators said to one another, "The government really is going to do it." So what do the speculators do in that case? They jump on top of the government speculation and all of a sudden, the rate started to go down much faster than the Government had intended it to go down.

Now the government was stuck. "We've got a tiger by the tail," they said. "How do we stop this downward slide of the rate?" When they initially started this operation, they had no intention of pegging the rate. What they were trying to do was drive it down.

When under their stimulus there was a rapid movement down, obviously the sensible thing for them to have done would have been to announce that they had made a mistake, that they were getting out of the market and that they were going to let the dollar resume its former behavior.

But no government in the world has ever done a thing like that. The key principle of a government is that you make a different mistake each time, not the same one. And you never admit that what you did before was wrong.

To go back, the only reason Canada got on a floating rate in the first place in 1950 was because of a similar earlier sequence in which they had made a mistake, when they had appreciated the Canadian pound earlier. And instead of undoing that mistake, they went on and floated. Well, similarly, this time, instead of simply undoing it, they said, "Well, the way we'll stop the rate from going down is by pegging it." So they announced that they were going to peg it at 92½ cents. As it happened, it took very large operations at that stage to break the speculative movement and to peg it. But they finally succeeded in pegging it at 92½ cents. Then they were stuck with it there.

It was a very unwise thing for them to do in terms of their own internal policy. It is not evidence in the slightest that the floating exchange rate wasn't working.

The Royal Bank of Canada has been a strong advocate of a floating rate in Canada and has published a considerable number of very interesting empirical analyses of the operations of it before and of the effects of freezing the rate afterwards.

Thanks to the exemption under the interest equalization tax which requires that Canada hold her foreign exchange holdings relatively constant, Canada is now pegged to the dollar in the literal sense. She is having a real gold standard in relation to the dollar. She is unifying her currency with the dollar.

MR. BRATTER: And at the annual meetings of the International Monetary Fund there is no country stronger than Canada for the system of fixed parities.

PROFESSOR FRIEDMAN: Of course! Why should this surprise you? They have to defend the action they took. When was the last time you heard an administrator get up and say, "Well now, the action I took was the wrong action for me to take"?

Do you hear that very often? The tyranny of the status quo is enormous.

When Canada first went on a floating rate in 1950, almost all of the banks of Canada were opposed to going on the floating rate. When Canada went off the floating rate in 1962, a considerable fraction of the banks were opposed to going off the floating rate. The basic principle of administration is that every administrator knows that the way he is conducting the particular program he is conducting is the only way it can be done. I was first taught this lesson in a very striking way back in 1941 to 1943 when I was working at the Treasury. I was involved in the development of the withholding system for personal income taxes.

If you asked Internal Revenue today whether they could collect the present income taxes without withholding at the source, there is no doubt that they would say it would be utterly impossible. But who was our biggest opponent when we tried to get withholding taxes in 1941 to 1943? Internal Revenue. They said it was unworkable, it was unfeasible, it was administratively not possible. So I think the fact that people who three years ago decided to shift to a fixed rate are defending the action they took is hardly evidence that the action they took was a wise action. I think the Canadian case is a very strong case on the other side, myself.

MR. SEGAL: As an interim step in reform, what would you think about widening the dollar gold point, let's say between $30 and $40 an ounce?

PROFESSOR FRIEDMAN: I think that would be a serious mistake. But I think widening the exchange rate limits would be very desirable. I would urge on you to separate the gold problem from the exchange rate problem. What we ought to do about gold, it seems to me, is a separate question from what we ought to do about exchange rates.

We could stop buying and selling gold and sit on it, let the gold price be a free market price like the price of lead or copper or anything else. And we could, as an interim matter, instead of having the pound pegged at $2.78 to $2.82, peg it between say $2.70 and $2.90. That would certainly be an improvement for exchange rates. But I think it is not a desirable thing to do it with gold.

MR. BRATTER: Prominent bankers recently suggested that the United States discontinue selling gold and there has been some speculation as to whether they were launching a trial balloon for the Secretary of the Treasury. If that were done, would we then be on floating rates?

PROFESSOR FRIEDMAN: No. As I tried to emphasize in my paper, there are two problems. If we unpegged silver, would that put us on floating rates? The problem of fixing the price of a commodity like gold or silver and the problem of pegging currencies are two separate problems.

Many countries — Germany and France — peg exchange rates. But they don't necessarily, as an official matter, peg the price of gold. In fact, in France you can buy and sell gold freely, but the price varies. The price of a French napoleon is not pegged.

So we could unpeg gold, stop buying and selling it, and yet continue to peg exchange rates for a considerable period.

MR. BRATTER: That is by official intervention, you mean.

PROFESSOR FRIEDMAN: That's what we do now.

How do we peg exchange rates now? We don't really do it by shipping gold.

MR. BRATTER: If we stopped buying gold and we did not peg—

PROFESSOR FRIEDMAN: Peg gold or peg exchange rates?

MR. BRATTER: Well, peg exchange rates.

PROFESSOR FRIEDMAN: Yes?

MR. BRATTER: Then what would be the initial effect of that step on the $2.82 rate for the pound sterling?

PROFESSOR FRIEDMAN: Well, in the case of the pound sterling, because Britain is in balance-of-payment difficulties, the pound sterling price would probably fall, not rise. What would happen would be that the dollar would very likely appreciate relative to the pound sterling, and depreciate relative to the franc and the mark.

So the different prices would behave in different ways. Trying to predict these things is much more complicated than it appears.

Let's suppose for a moment that tomorrow we eliminated the interest equalization tax and all our voluntary exchange controls. Let's suppose we eliminated oil import quotas and a bunch of the other quotas, and let's suppose we set the dollar free.

I am not sure that the dollar would fall. It might temporarily. But I'm talking about what would happen over six months or a year. Do you suppose that when a bank has lots of outstanding liabilities and that banker gets on the stairs of his bank and says, "You know, we're a very sound bank, but, gee, I wish you would hold off coming in and trying to ask to get your deposits for six months or a year." Do you think that's the way to strengthen confidence in that bank? I don't think so.

Similarly, we have been doing everything we possibly could to weaken confidence in the dollar and to tell everybody in the world, "You're a fool if you hold onto any more dollars than you have to."

If we acted from strength, which we have—and simply said, "We're going to stop all this nonsense, we're going to remove the interest equalization tax, we're not going to force our military to buy on the most expensive market and so on," I would not be a bit surprised if the market price of the dollar strengthened rather than weakened.

You know, it's an interesting thing that economic events often work very much differently than you expect.

What killed silver as a monetary metal? The fact that we raised its price.

That seems kind of paradoxical, doesn't it?

MR. BRATTER: No. Silver — the silver standard started to disappear in the last century. We just—

PROFESSOR FRIEDMAN: Yes, to some extent it did.

MR. BRATTER: India went off the silver standard in 1893.

PROFESSOR FRIEDMAN: Yes. But when did China go off it?

MR. BRATTER: China went off when we started buying silver heavily in 1934.

PROFESSOR FRIEDMAN: Right.

MR. BRATTER: That's when they officially went off.

PROFESSOR FRIEDMAN: Right. What happened to Mexico?

MR. BRATTER: Mexico went off much earlier.

PROFESSOR FRIEDMAN: But Mexico still had an extensive full-bodied silver coinage. What happened to it in 1934?

MR. BRATTER: It went to the melting pot after we started buying.

PROFESSOR FRIEDMAN: Right. If we had not engaged in a silver-purchase program in 1934, silver would today be a monetary metal.

What killed gold as a monetary metal?

MR. BRATTER: I wouldn't follow you on that.

PROFESSOR FRIEDMAN: What killed gold as a monetary metal is that we raised the price to $35 an ounce in 1934 and accompanied that by measures making it illegal for individuals to hold gold and in effect declaring gold clauses unenforceable. Paradoxically, that is what killed gold as a monetary metal. And that is why the gold standard at the moment can only be re-established, if ever, by first getting rid of the vestiges of it that we now have and letting it re-emerge as a real honest-to-God gold standard.

MR. SEGAL: To come back to the point about widening the gold points, would you agree with this chain of events which I deduce logically? That if we were to widen the gold points and therefore made it risky for a country like France to hold gold, then France would have the choice of either continuing to peg on the dollar—which she now does—or pegging on gold.

If she chose to peg on gold, would she have flexible exchange rates?

PROFESSOR FRIEDMAN: That's right.

MR. SEGAL: I mean would you accept this as a strategy that might help to put us on the right road?

PROFESSOR FRIEDMAN: Well, I don't know. Maybe.

I was directing my attention to the question of whether it was desirable to keep the gold as a means through which you adjusted exchange rates.

Your idea would be to let the gold price be determined on the London gold market?

MR. SEGAL: Yes.

PROFESSOR FRIEDMAN: And to peg it between $30 and $40 an ounce?

MR SEGAL: Yes. With plenty of play.

PROFESSOR FRIEDMAN: Well, maybe if it went up to $40 an ounce and we could get rid of most of our gold at that price, it might be worth doing. It's better than getting rid of it at $35 an ounce.

You see, I must say that my own favorite scheme is completely impossible politically, and therefore I'm not talking about it. But if you were being rational, the rational thing—and this is supposed to be a rational debate—in my opinion for the United States to do would be first:

Repeal all prohibitions on private individuals owning gold, trading in gold, or exchanging gold.

Second, announce that on one Monday we are going to have an auction and we're going to get rid of the gold stock to the highest bidder and go out of the business.

I see no reason why the storage of gold should be a nationalized industry, any more than I see why the delivery of mail should be a nationalized industry. They are equally illogical, and we see the inefficient results in both cases.

But, as I say, I realize that this is highly unfeasible politically. So I have been inclined to content myself with saying, "Okay, let's stop buying and selling gold and just sit on our gold stock."

As a political matter maybe your device would be a better one for getting off. I really haven't thought about that particular device.

MR. BRATTER: Are there many Milton Friedmans abroad advocating this sort of thing?

PROFESSOR FRIEDMAN: It depends on what you mean by "this sort of thing." If you mean by "this sort of thing" more flexibility in exchange rates, the situation today is that if you were to poll the professional people in money and international trade, the academic people, you will find that at least three-quarters of them are in favor of a greater degree of flexibility of exchange rates.

This is a tremendous change in opinion. Fifteen to 20 years ago you would not have found 5 percent.

But today I don't think there is the slightest doubt that an overwhelming majority of people in this area would favor a greater degree of flexibility of exchange rates.

Not all of them would go to completely floating rates. Most probably would not.

Most people would favor widening the range of fluctuation and seeing how that worked. Some people would go to a more complicated system of widening the range and having a movable peg, saying that in any year in which the exchange rate is toward the lower end of the band the parity rates would be lowered. That would be a possible in-between case. That is, so far as the academic world is concerned.

If you go to the financial community, the number of people who are in favor of flexible exchange rates or floating exchange rates is many fewer. That's understandable, I think. This is their business. And everybody is always in favor of free prices for everybody else, but not for himself.

MR. BRATTER: That is especially true if they get a phone call from Washington.

PROFESSOR FRIEDMAN: Yes, I'm sure that's right.

That is part of the problem in this area. It is impossible for any high official to hint at the possibility that exchange rates might be changed. And understandably.

If I were a high official, I wouldn't hint at it so long as the government is committed to holding it. Therefore it is very difficult to get an intelligent, open public debate on this issue. It has to come entirely from the outside.

For example, a couple of years ago the Council of Economic Advisers professed in one section of its report to discuss all the alternative ways in which you might adjust the balance of payments. They said, "We're not talking about policy, we're just going to give the economics of it." Yet that section did not contain the words "exchange rate." It obviously was not a scientific discussion. It was understandably, but nonetheless actually, a political discussion.

If you will pardon me for saying so, I think the banking community is being extremely shortsighted because it seems to me that it would be in their interest to move toward floating rates. Here they are, accepting ever-increasing controls over their business, controls over whom they may lend to abroad and at what terms. Why? For what gain to themselves? They are the people who could specialize in this business of foreign exchange transactions. Who would it be who would run the futures markets?

MR. BRATTER: Did you notice that the Bankers Association of Foreign Trade just this week protested against this?

PROFESSOR FRIEDMAN: Maybe, but that doesn't make them any the less shortsighted. I am an empirical scientist. In many other areas I have observed time and again that the business community, in these issues of public policy, is very shortsighted. Time and again, they oppose measures which, after they are adopted, they welcome.

We had a very simple recent case of this, the investment credit. As it happens, I have always been opposed to the investment credit. I think it's a bad tax measure. It should never have been on the books. When it was first proposed the business community at large was violently opposed to it.

Last year, when it was proposed to take it off, the business community said this was the greatest thing that had ever happened and that it was disgraceful to take it off. This is one example. But there are numerous other examples of the fact that the business community in this respect tends to be very shortsighted. If it is true that banks engaging in foreign trade came out against floating exchange rates, it's another—

MR. BRATTER: I'm not saying that. They came out against all of these controls that you have mentioned.

PROFESSOR FRIEDMAN: I beg your pardon. I thought you said against floating rates.

MR. BRATTER: Oh, no, no, no.

PROFESSOR FRIEDMAN: But what is their alternative? There is no point in coming out against these controls unless you have an alternative.

MR. BRATTER: I couldn't tell you. I didn't see the full statement.

PROFESSOR FRIEDMAN: Otherwise they are just spitting into the wind. Unless you have some alternative adjustment mechanism, you must have direct or indirect exchange controls. There is no alternative. There's no use kidding yourself. You cannot have your cake and eat it too.

Under present circumstances in the world, you cannot have fixed rates and freedom from control indefinitely. You can have it for a time, but you can't indefinitely.

PROFESSOR PAUL McCRACKEN, University of Michigan: I have just a comment on this. I think the Bankers Association, or this statement, probably was opting for what really would be the kind of austerity program that the British have—in other words, to try to take the adjustment in the form of a lower level of business activity.

PROFESSOR FRIEDMAN: Again, if that is so, it's another evidence of shortsightedness. What do they gain from that? Is it really in the self-interest of the banking community to force a recession on this country in order to enable the price of the mark, let's say, in terms of the dollar to be kept at 25 cents?

What is there about this particular price that makes it a be-all and end-all of policy? I think the explanation is that the alternative has not been made clear to them. If they examined the alternatives and if they had the choice of either a slight fluctuation in the price of the dollar in terms of foreign exchange or a substantial recession or depression in this country, it's very hard for me to see how anybody could opt for the second under present circumstances.

MR. BRATTER: I think you have to distinguish between two kinds of bankers. We have a certain number of large banks which are engaged in international activity and the rest of the 14,000 banks in this country are domestically oriented and know very little about this excepting what they hear from the leaders.

PROFESSOR FRIEDMAN: Yes.

MR. BRATTER: They have no original ideas on it.

PROFESSOR FRIEDMAN: I'm sure you're right.

PROFESSOR McCRACKEN: Both groups tend to agree on this.

PROFESSOR FRIEDMAN: As Paul says, both the large banks and the small banks tend to agree?

MR. BRATTER: That's what I say, they get their leaders, who lead the way.

PROFESSOR FRIEDMAN: Then it's the large banks who need to be educated on this issue.

MR. SEGAL: Just one footnote. I think that in the case of these large banks really what they were for, and I can document this in the case of the interest equalization tax, was a corporative system of controls. They were opposed to the interest equalization tax in 1963. What they really wanted was a capital issues committee. They are all for that.

PROFESSOR FRIEDMAN: Sure, I don't blame them.

MR. SEGAL: This could be a cozy cartel.

PROFESSOR FRIEDMAN: Let me go back. One of the reasons why the bigger banks have ambiguous attitudes is because, of course, the so-called voluntary agreement to restrict foreign lending is simply a cartel agreement.

MR. SEGAL: Of course.

PROFESSOR FRIEDMAN: Under which they can charge higher prices to foreign borrowers than they otherwise could and under which they are protected from competition of people who are not in the business.

MR. SEGAL: Exactly.

PROFESSOR FRIEDMAN: As you all realize, the President asked and received a legislative exemption from the Antitrust Act in order to make this voluntary restriction on foreign lending effective. So they had mixed motives.

On the one hand, their cartel interests led them to favor it but again I think this is shortsighted. They may, in the short run, get something out of this cartel but, as exchange controls tighten up, they are going to find that the cartel is not operated in the way in which their own interests would dictate. But maybe I'm wrong. Maybe the cartel is in their own interest. Well, then it is up to the rest of us to whose interests it is adverse to try to do something about it.

MR. BRATTER: Well, the additional charge which is represented by the tax does not go to the banker.

PROFESSOR FRIEDMAN: No, no. Not the Interest Equalization Tax. I am talking about the voluntary agreement on bank lending. There is no charge on that.

JAROSLAV HABR, Academy of Sciences, Prague, Czechoslovakia: Is it not an advantage for people who are engaged in long-term planning to have fixed prices? Otherwise, in addition to all the other uncertainties, they are also subject to uncertainty about prices.

PROFESSOR FRIEDMAN: These people are faced with a risky situation with fixed prices. If the prices are fixed wrong, then something else is unstable. Again, it seems to me what is involved in that argument is the belief that you can have your cake and eat it too.

Of course, it would be very nice if you could have stable prices and also the equality of supply and demand in all markets, but you cannot, if conditions are changing. You can fix the price, but then you have to do something else about the quantity. You may have greater stability in prices, perhaps under an arrangement with fixed prices but you have greater uncertainty about everything else. And, in fact, the long-term planners are in a far better position, if they have the flexible and prompt signal of prices to give them information about the state of demand and supply in various markets, than if they have to infer themselves that state of demand and supply from the length of queues of various kinds. That's very complicated to do.

Just consider in this country for a moment, leave aside Czechoslovakia and Poland, consider in this country the situation in agriculture. Look at the problem our agricultural planners have been up against. Why? Because they don't have a price system to do the job for them and they are trying to do crudely what this much more effective instrument would do in a sensitive way.

If, in fact, internal monetary policy in the United States is stable and in other countries is stable, then, under a system of floating exchange rates, exchange rates will be free to move but they will, in fact, be highly stable.

The price of sugar is free to move in our markets but it's highly stable. The prices of other products which are free to move are highly stable. There is a difference between being free to move and actually moving around a lot. And, if the price does actually move around a lot, it's because something is happening to move it. That something would still be there if you froze the price.

DR. HABR: May I comment?

PROFESSOR FRIEDMAN: Sure, I would like to have you.

DR. HABR: Because it seems to me that there is a difference, if you can make your decisions on the ground of the development of prices on a free market. So it's not so difficult to take into consideration the various factors which involve your field of activity. But if besides this you must take into consideration, let's say, this movement of exchange rates in a country, then you don't know what are the real reasons for these changes. They are connected with various factors which are not necessarily within your own sphere of activity.

PROFESSOR FRIEDMAN: Right, right, right.

DR. HABR: So it's much more risky a situation —

PROFESSOR FRIEDMAN: No, no, it's the other way around. If I don't have the exchange rates moving, if they are pegged, then I really have to go and find out about those real things. But, if the exchange rates are moving, then they give me the information without my knowing the real things. I don't have to know why the exchange rate is rising. You say to me, "Well, I have to know whether it's going to be higher a year from now." Fine, I have a futures market on which specialists in exchange rates speculate. They provide me, free, for no cost, with information that I could never in a hundred years get myself by trying to become an expert in all these different areas.

The great virtue of a price system, and it's just as much a virtue in exchange as it is in other areas, is that it's an extremely effective way of giving each man the information he needs.

How am I going to get that information some other way? Suppose I freeze the exchange rate? I still have to know whether it's going to be possible ten years from now, if I invest now in Brazil, to get my dollars out. If I have frozen exchange rates, I have to ask myself, ten years from now will Brazil be in a situation where exchange control will be loose enough so they will permit me to take my dollars out? I submit that's a much harder thing to forecast than it is simply to sell some dollars forward on a forward exchange market.

DR. HABR: It is the sort of argumentation that this would be better than the present type, which is worse, but it is not an argumentation that either is right.

PROFESSOR FRIEDMAN: What's a better one? Tell me a better one?

DR. HABR: Oh, yes, with that I quite agree. We are in a tight situation.

PROFESSOR FRIEDMAN: The truth is that the future is uncertain. That's the truth. Now, the question is, among alternative mechanisms for dealing with uncertainty, which one comes closest to giving the right answer? None can give the right answer because the future is unknowable. It really is uncertain. Among the various mechanisms that imperfect men have invented or that have grown up, the price system seems to be about the most efficient as a transmitter of information and as a means whereby people can deal with true uncertainty.

And I think the problem is the one you have suggested. Everybody wants to have his cake and eat it too. He wants to have a fixed exchange rate and also always have the freedom to buy and sell an unlimited amount of exchange and also have stable prices internally and externally.

He can't. Something has to give and, therefore, you have to choose which is the thing that it is best to have give.

SECOND SESSION

PROFESSOR HENRY BRIEFS, Georgetown University: I want to get to the question of adjustment in the balance of payments under conditions of pegged exchange rates. This view of the way in which balance can be restored has a lot of appeal. I think it has been part of the central doctrine about the adjustment mechanism under pegged rates.

One of the difficulties is that you have to accept variations in the unemployment rate. That is, if you vary the growth rate, you are going to get fluctuations in the unemployment rate. Unfortunately, because of domestic considerations, countries have tied themselves down to rather rigid criteria of what an acceptable unemployment rate is. If you are willing to let the unemployment rate fluctuate, let's say, in our case, between 3.7 and 4.5 percent, this might make some sense.

But, if you get the view, which you are beginning to get, that any time the unemployment rate moves towards 4 percent or possibly beyond that we really have a recession underway, balance-of-payments adjustments in terms of variations in the growth rate seems to go down the drain. In other words, if you are rigidly tied to maintaining a very low level of unemployment, you can't have such flexibility in the growth rate and you just paralyze the adjustment mechanism.

DR. ROOSA: The best answer is to say that there will always have to be some range of variation in the unemployment rate, as a byproduct of the change that is always going to be underway within a dynamic domestic economy. Whatever is found by experience to be the acceptable range of unemployment required by purely domestic adjustments should set the outer limits on what is produced by any action considered necessary for balance-of-payments adjustments.

That isn't a clear and resounding answer in terms of percentages. There are people who will still raise questions as to whether for domestic reasons at times the rate may have to go as high as 4.5 percent. We will be refining these criteria over the years ahead as we already have in the recent past.

I can remember vividly a time when some of my associates and I thought we were talking about pie in the sky when we tried to visualize a set of arrangements that would lead to 4 percent unemployment and, at the same time, bring this about in an environment of relative price stability and thereby also be helpful to the balance of payments.

I think, if we keep this same objective, we will find as the unemployment target is further sharpened over the years, as we learn more about the intractable or malleable nature of the composition of the remaining unemployment, that we'll be able to make the necessary balance-of-payments adjustments without necessarily increasing unemployment beyond that range of fluctuation which would be implied and inevitable for the viability of a dynamic economy.

I think that can even be said about the thinking of some of the people in the United Kingdom and the change that they've induced to increase the unemployment rate to 2 percent. I don't myself agree that such an objective was inevitable. I think the British government was drawn to this (relatively mild) extremity because it didn't take other kinds of appropriate balance-of-payments action earlier. This is only to highlight, though, the need all of us face to make the judgments in advance that we could have made better in retrospect.

But I don't think there has to be anything inherently contradictory here, between my suggestion for varying the rate of economic advance and the widespread commitments to hold unemployment at low levels. What I'm suggesting is going to be harder, because it's a very simple and easy prescription to be brutal and to say, we'll take the unemployment, we'll rattle things around and we'll bust through in a hurry. My way is going to have to be longer and slower moving, but I don't see any fundamental reason why, if we are convinced of the objectives, the engineering of it can't be brought about.

HARVEY SEGAL, *Washington Post:* Two questions, really.

The first one is: What are the grounds for your confidence that the adjustments under a system of fixed exchange rates can be confined to, first differences, all of them positive in the rate of output? I think I could argue that the experience from 1958 to 1961 doesn't support your case.

Secondly, what about the very serious problems of forecasting, if we are going to continue along the lines that you are suggesting? And I am thinking of the situation that confronts the country at this moment. In view of your appraisal of the balance-of-payments outlook, what sort of domestic policy would you advocate?

I am curious to know because I am wondering if they are not in conflict.

DR. ROOSA: As to the first, I can't introduce any proof. There is no necessary reason, of course, why all of the changes are going to work out in such a way that there will only be variations in the quarter-by-quarter pluses, as between larger or smaller figures in the process of achieving adjustment.

I do say that this is a reasonable aim of economic policy and that I think most of the time it should be workable. The demonstration of it is going to be limited or the evidence is going to be limited by our success in reasonable fulfillment of the challenge posed by your second question and there will always be room for human error there too.

The forecasting problem for any purpose, whether that of a completely insular economy or that of one exposed to the outside world, is always difficult. Even so, the spillage that we have to contemplate for the balance of payments of the United States, however important that may be now because we have run deficits for so long, is, in our case, relatively much smaller than for any other country.

But I do feel that the need—in accepting what I regard as the premises of modern economics or as Arthur Okun says, "good economics"—the need is to make the forecasting art one that is continually being improved. This need exists and persists for the domestic economy. Folding into any forecast the foreign economic policy implications—choosing from among a variety of choices, those choices that will also be most useful in balance-of-payments terms—seems to me relatively the easier part of the process.

Now, to take the immediate situation and the balance-of-payments difficulty that we face, I have no better figures than those of the first quarter, but I am assuming that we are now running, on a conventional basis, a balance-of-payments deficit of over $2 billion at an annual rate and that this is going to require some repair action and some corrective action.

The corrective action broadly is the same that I think is needed for the continued strength and advance of the home economy and for absorbing the continued increase in the labor force. I think that does mean that we first will benefit from the restoration of the investment credit and the stimulus to productivity-raising investment that this provides. Second, that, and here I am being very brash and without any analysis am just trying to give illustrations which any of you can improve upon but, second, I think we are going to have to rely, if the expansion becomes a problem on the inflationary side (with the continued growth of Vietnam expenditure) we are going to have to rely more on overall tax increases.

That means that, as of now, my guess would be that a recommendation should be made for a tax surcharge, that the timing will be a little later than originally contemplated, probably by the 1st of October but no later as an effective date than the 1st of January. Based on information neither you nor I have, and I don't suppose Mr. McNamara has yet but will soon have to have, on the scale of the further increments on the expenditure side, I would feel that there is a risk that this will have to be a 10 percent, not a 6 percent surcharge, and I would think that accompanying that there will be some slowing down in the pace of monetary expansion that has proceeded so rapidly in the early months of this year; that will still mean an expansion in the magnitudes of these days that is within the bounds of a normal seasonal growth.

I doubt that it's possible to drive the whole structure of interest rates very much lower, because the economy itself will be so strong that you will be fighting an irresistible force, if you try to contrive rates which don't equate supply and demand in the market. But the same balancing of the components of fiscal and monetary

measures, and the same need for restraint in the series
of large wage negotiations ahead of us, that will be necessary for domestic balance and growth will also be
appropriate for improving our own competitive position
balance-of-payments wise.

I suppose it's unlikely that anything we do can accomplish a reduction in the rate of price increase below
2.5 percent and we may get something more this year;
but I think, even at that, we may gain ground in the
competitive race, balance-of-payments wise, around the
world. I also think the fact that we have passed the
period of peak inventory accumulations and should now,
certainly by the next quarter, be proceeding at a rate
which is more nearly normal in comparison with sales
advances, perhaps still a little on the low side, will in
turn mean that that volume of marginal demand which
reaches outside the country and produces an increase in
imports will not be present. The economy will still ex-
pand but the high ratio of import increases that often
accompanies an extraordinary rise in inventories will not
be present.

And I would then think that we should see for this
year an improvement on the trade account in the magnitude of one-half to one billion dollars, all of which
will be lost on the other side through Vietnam expenditure and through some further slippage on the capital
outflow with the result that the total ordinary liquidity
deficit will run somewhat higher than last year. And,
just because the Euro-dollar market plays a role here too,

the deficit on the official settlements basis this year will probably be higher than the liquidity deficit. That doesn't worry me a bit.

I do think, insofar as this is a problem, that the important thing is that the holding of the additional dollars flowing from this operation will end up either in the IMF through other transactions or in Germany where, at least, there is a kind of contented holding, or in the countries on the periphery of Vietnam who are interested in rebuilding their reserves.

So that I think, with the present combination of developments and Treasury tactics, we can now avoid the kind of balance-of-payments problem that has any explosive connotations this year. But next year will be another story.

NORMAN TURE, National Bureau of Economic Research: I would like to pursue the same line of questioning that Henry Briefs and Harvey Segal have initiated but, Dr. Roosa, I first want to offer a comment, if I may, on your tax prescriptions.

The restoration of the investment credit ought to reduce the tax on the returns to corporate capital by something of the order of $2 billion. The proposed increase in corporate taxes under a 6 percent surcharge proposal would be something of the order of magnitude of $3 billion. It is hard for me to see why this represents a combination of measures that will, in fact, increase the incentive for investment in productivity-enhancing capital in the corporate sector.

But may I now ask my question?

DR. ROOSA: Certainly. I am going to treat that as a question too, if you don't mind.

MR. TURE: All right.

It seems to me that when you make the observation that one virtue of a fixed-exchange system is that it sends up clues when a payments deficit occurs and indicates what should be done to domestic policy, underlying that there has got to be some sort of assumption that the change in the deficit in either direction is a function of the rate of resource utilization in the domestic economy.

But it seems to me that the experience of the late 1950s and the early 1960s does not confirm that. What was happening then, if memory serves me correctly, was that the unemployment rate was high, well above 5 percent, that prices were quite stable, and that our balance-of-payments deficits were intractable.

Furthermore, is it not so that the reliance on a fixed-exchange system had the effect of making us minimize domestic expansionary policies and when at last we saw fit to pursue somewhat more expansionary policies than we otherwise would have, this forced us to such exotic manipulations in the money markets as Operation Twist and exhortations to the private business community to inhibit their investments abroad? This is hardly one of the virtues of a fixed-exchange system; that is, it hardly tends toward improvement in capital allocation internationally.

DR. ROOSA: The answer to all of your questions is that everything is relative and nothing is perfect.

But, first, on your point about the tax impact, actually we don't have just one monolithic corporation which pays all the taxes. If, in an environment in which taxes are increasing, there are some who have an opportunity of getting a remission of tax by taking certain action, they have every incentive to take the action and the incentive that is indicated by the investment credit is that of, hopefully, adding to the stock of productive, creative capital in the economy.

So that I don't see any problem of inconsistency there.

On the one side, given a composition of output which is underway, there is a need for an incentive which will exert some influence on the composition of that output in the direction of increasing the productive capability of the economy—a little more going toward investment, within the total of all resources being used for all purposes.

Given the total that is available for all purposes, considerably more also has to be devoted to meeting government expenses in a period when otherwise the aggregate of demand would itself add to additional inflationary pressures which, I assume, you wouldn't want to see for domestic reasons.

When translating any of this into balance-of-payments terms, I think there is a built-in tendency to want to "think simple." I would enjoy doing so. But in this area, perhaps because I'm defending what we have, I can't. There simply cannot be the direct and one-way sort of a tradeoff that is implied in your formulation— at least not often.

Now, the United States' situation in the late fifties was, of course, a special one. It didn't fit any of the books because we had a balance-of-payments deficit at the same time that we had a very large current account surplus. And still do. We, therefore, had to look for the cause in the behavior of capital movements and transfers. The nature of the forces at work was such that if there had been further reductions of interest rates, as such, at that time, more money would have flowed out. Actually, without reductions in short rates, indeed while they were rising, there were continuing increases in the availability and directed used of borrowed funds and it proved possible to influence their allocation constructively, without worsening the deficit in our balance of payments. If there had simply been the technique of flooding out liquidity and then letting it spill wherever it would go, the consequences would have been greater outflows balance-of-payments wise. We might have been able to sponge some of them up, as we did sponge up much of what did flow anyway, but probably with more difficulty.

We didn't have to make that choice. There were other ways of accomplishing what we wanted for the domestic economy in an orderly manner and in a lasting way that also held great promise for the balance of payments.

And here is an alibi if you have ever heard one, but

in 1964, if it had not been for the capital outflow problem which we had still not fully resolved (and which had taken on new characteristics of its own) the response to the whole program initiated in 1961 and worked out over the next three years, the response to that whole program had by 1964, along with a lot of good luck, produced a balance-of-payments surplus on current account that could have covered all of our outflows. As you remember, the current account surplus, conservatively measured, was well over $7 billion. This was achieved when the economy had, at the same time, been rapidly expanding, the most rapid expansion we had had in ages, and when unemployment was being absorbed.

We devised a program that had some chance of working in that environment toward the resolution of both problems—unemployment at home and deficits abroad. There were slippages along the way to be sure, but as a conception of a program I still don't have any regrets about the way in which that was designed. I am in no position, however, to be an apologist for the period that just preceded it.

I would say that out of the experience of that preceding period a good many lessons were learned and we are still, I hope, all of us learning them. I doubt that it will ever be possible to say that balance-of-payments problems exist for the United States just because there is something wrong with the rate of resource utilization in the United States, as you put it. That may or may not be what a balance-of-payments problem at any given moment points to.

But certainly in the early sixties we did have a problem of utilizing resources and we attempted to develop a combination of measures that would not only increase the resource utilization but would reduce the deficits. While the deficits certainly have continued each year due to some other proximate cause, the nature of the problem as it existed in 1961 was not intractable and the problem as it existed in 1961 was solved in 1964.

We live in a dynamic world and you can't always foresee all of the next year's problems. But the new problems then were essentially those on the capital side. To say that a free-rate system, as of that time, when capital was flowing out at a rapid rate, could have been helpful is to me inconceivable.

Now, I know what Professor Friedman says. He said it in his testimony before the Joint Economic Committee in 1963. I was still down here, then, and I had to try to imagine what his prescription would mean.

The outflow of capital, if it had been able to reflect itself in a flexible rate, would have cut the United States dollar exchange rate against other countries very sharply. Exports from the United States would have become much less costly to others, not just by pennies but (in the magnitudes of that time) by dimes and quarters. Other countries could not have tolerated massive increases in their imports and would have taken retaliatory defensive measures. Meanwhile, with supplies of our goods for export not wholly elastic, their domestic prices in the United States would have begun running up—disrupting our own domestic price stability.

How was that going to solve the problem that we were confronting at that time? It seems to me it's absolutely upside down. I still can't see what it was he had in mind but perhaps next week he'll explain.

DANIEL EDWARDS, Joint Economic Committee: I would like to follow up the ideas of Norm and Harvey.

As a side observation, the stock of money right now is less than 1 percent above where it was last year and although most of the econometric models that are being used indicate the economy might roar in the last half of this year, most of these models are not very sensitive to money and credit conditions.

You hinted that a more elastic view of gold wouldn't lead to the end of the world, as many people have suggested. I am wondering what the pattern of events would have been after 1958, if the United States had gone off of gold internationally as well as domestically in the thirties?

DR. ROOSA: There are a lot of different meanings about going off gold. I'll try to take that one quickly first.

Bernard Baruch used to call me up every few weeks in the days when we first had some thought of taking off the gold cover back early—I've forgotten now, 1961 sometime — and he always referred to that as going off gold and he was terribly worried about it.

The assumption that I am making about your statement is that you mean by "going off gold" that we simply ceased either to buy or sell.

MR. EDWARDS: That is correct.

DR. ROOSA: And maintained no price.

MR. EDWARDS: That's correct.

DR. ROOSA: We would use it if we found a chance to auction it off to meet a balance-of-payments deficit sometime but it would have served no role in the world monetary system.

MR. EDWARDS: That's right.

DR. ROOSA: In that case, we would now, in my view, be living in a world in which Hjalmar Schacht would be very much at home.

MR. EDWARDS: But what do you think the sequence of events would have been internationally after 1958?

DR. ROOSA: We just wouldn't have had the convertibility change that occurred in 1958, there couldn't have been the move. The result then would have been that much of what provided the currency environment for the really fabulous expansion of internal and external trade over the past decade—the fixed certainty of being able to do business at known prices and reasonably lasting values—would have been gone.

There would have been nothing that the world monetary system could hold to as an anchor for the fixed-rate system. In time there would have been the evolution of a dollar bloc and a good many countries would have joined it. Within the dollar bloc we would be permitting relatively free capital movement to those who were members of it, and none, except perhaps through centralized licensing, to those who were outside. As to what would have happened to those outside, anybody could conjure up a dozen schemes.

But the evolution of a dollar bloc itself, once we went off gold, would just consist of those countries which, in order to have some element of certainty, said they'd be willing to set a fixed exchange rate with the dollar, that they would invoice their transactions with others in the group in dollars, and stay with us, provided that they would have access to our capital market.

This dollar bloc, I suppose, would have included all of Latin America very quickly, and much of the less developed part of the world, where the capacity for developing capital needs is enormous. There would have to be some scheme I think of priorities and queuing, as has developed, as far as I know, in every other bloc system that has been developed.

I am not just trying to create a horrendous picture here. I am trying to give you a quick answer as to what I think would have happened. That is why I was so concerned to see that it didn't happen when I had a little chance to begin dealing with the question at the end of 1960.

As you may remember, there was widespread expectation that it might happen as soon as President Kennedy came in. This is why I didn't go to anything more than the swearing in on Inauguration Day and was on the phone in touch with the gold market all that day. Then subsequently, of course, over the weekend there was no problem, and things settled down thereafter. But some of the traders in critically sensitive parts of the world were all ready for a real run on gold. They expected, in that event, that we would have to split off into some kind of a defensive dollar bloc system. The more gold they had, the better their bargaining position would then be because they could always sell it for something in the trade they had with the United States. And it would give them time to decide whether or not, at least, they wanted to join such a bloc.

As to the other question that you asked, the more immediate one, that the money supply is only up 1 percent above last year, the question of the choice of dates is always a problem there. I am not close enough to the details. I have the luxury of knowing so little that I can have strong views.

I do feel that it is not likely that the rate of increase that has prevailed since November can continue. That rate, I think, and I may be wrong here, but I think at an annual rate the increase in the money supply over that period has been somewhere in the area approaching 5 percent,[1] and I would think we have made enough recovery now from that gushing so that the continuing increase will be at a somewhat slower rate.

I would be surprised, though, if we ended up with an increase in the money supply, strictly defined, of less than somewhere in the 3 percent area on an average for this year as a whole over last year.

From what I know, and it isn't much, I think that would be about right.

MR. EDWARDS: I agree with you. The problem is that, if you follow it, the money supply has decreased the last four weeks and, although that is too short a period to set a trend, you can get concerned when the administration is known to be looking at the econometric models and believing that the explosion is going to take place sometime in the third or fourth quarter.

You can interpret this recent contraction as evidence that the Fed has already reversed policy in anticipation of an inflation. It could be a case of again over-reacting.

DR. ROOSA: No, I doubt it. My hunch would be that, even though this is a time in which the more rapid rate of increase in money supply can appropriately slow down, at the same time, with the prospect of what I would regard as appropriate fiscal action, at least in the wings, I would not think that this is a situation in which the Fed needs to be thinking for balance-of-payments reasons or any other reasons in restrictive terms.

Getting back to a position of nourishing a good average growth rate, I would think, if it becomes a problem of inflationary pressure, at this stage (and I certainly can be wrong, these are things that need the combined judgment of dozens of people all debating all the time and on the basis of some knowledge, which I don't have) I would think that this will be the time when the emphasis ought to be on the general tax side.

I did promise a reply to this chap here—I know we're getting up to the time limit but I made a promise I had better go through with.

PROFESSOR EDWARD MURPHY, Georgetown University: Thank you. I had the feeling that part of your defense of fixed rates was based on some of the problems associated with flexible rates. One of these had to do with capital movements. I believe you suggested that under the system of fixed rates capital tended to be internationally distributed in a more economic way than it would under flexible rates.

I am not so sure that this is immediately obvious but I believe that the history of fixed rates, at least since World War I, has been that governments have not really permitted capital flows to be as large as they probably would have in the absence of controls.

We see today a large number of controls, formal and informal, being instituted by the United States government. The controls which exist in Europe, even today, on capital flows are known. While we don't restrict private capital flow too much to underdeveloped countries, I would assume we might if they got very large. We certainly do restrict government capital flows to underdeveloped countries through AID.

I really wonder the extent to which this is a viable criticism of flexible rates. Perhaps in the private capital flows which do take place under fixed rates, there is some assurance of a future return, but isn't the relevant comparison really the capital flows that don't take place because of the controls?

DR. ROOSA: You are going to think that I can only play one broken record, but the same answer is that we have to make comparisons between degrees of inadequacy rather than assume that either approach could assume the total fulfillment of some of these objectives. I think the key is in what you said about the fact that with fixed rates there is a readier opportunity to make the calculations on which a rational allocation of capital around the world can be accomplished.

Now, the fact that governments interfere with this is a fact of life that we have to deal with on its own. This only illustrates that that system is better which is at least geared to the assumption that governments will stay out and not to the assumption that governments must always be in the market, in a significant way. I take a "flexible," though not a "free," system to mean that governments will always be jiggling or at least influencing the current movement of exchange rates.

My feeling is that we would have found the same governmental aim of restricting capital movements under any system. Governments were restricting capital flows before they nominally went convertible. They defined convertibility in the Monetary Fund way back in the war period as meaning only current account transactions. They never wanted to have capital move freely. This is a big question. It's built into a great proportion of the history of investment and development around the world.

And, in my view, the framework in which you have a greater opportunity, at least, to urge, press, and plead for some freeing of the governmental restrictions and thereby allow the private allocation process to work, is the fixed-rate system.

The fact that the United States has fallen from grace in this respect after years of pleading with others to look toward virtue is, without alibiing too much, the result of the fact that even we weren't big enough to go it alone, completely alone, on the road of freedom for capital movements, and what we have done has still very carefully—with the exception of certain provisions to favor the less developed countries, as you mentioned—all been designed to retain the freedom of judgment of the source of capital here as to where it should go, where it can be most productive, and where the earnings can be greatest.

You may not believe it, but that's the same theory on which the interest equalization tax was devised: that government action would just raise the cost of putting money in a foreign country and then, with the cost generalized, it would be up to the investor to decide where the investment goes, if it goes.

So that the whole notion of our restrictions, undesirable and unfortunate as they are, has still been consistent with the allocative principle that is possible under a fixed-rate system. That is the allocation according to where on the basis of a reasonable calculation, you can earn the most over time. I don't see anything wrong with that if you believe in a market economy.

JAROSLAV HABR, Academy of Sciences, Prague, Czechoslovakia: After hearing you and Professor Murphy and Professor Milton Friedman and the gentleman who raised the last question, I am rather puzzled.

DR. ROOSA: No wonder.

DR. HABR: It seems to me that the difference is more in the meaning of the words fixed and flexible than in reality. For your fixed rates are practically flexible and Professor Friedman's flexible rates are in reality fixed.

But I would like to know if the real point of difference is that according to your view you would like to adjust the internal situation between the development of economies to the rate of exchange; whereas, according to the view of Professor Friedman, the rates ought to be adjusted to the development of individual economies.

DR. ROOSA: This is a very profound way of putting a difference which is rather confused, as you first noted.

There are formulations that I have seen of Professor Friedman's that would correspond to the point you have made, that he thinks in terms of letting the rate, the external rate, adjust so that you can devote yourself fully to the domestic economy.

In that sense I, perhaps unfairly, extend this in an exaggerated way to say, if you accomplish that (and I don't think the United States can, but perhaps other countries can) then you really are successfully using the rate to build a wall of isolation around your own country.

It's understandable that that could be chosen as an aim of policy. But I am a multilateralist. I feel that the distribution of resources around the world—always somewhat haphazard and always lagging and subject to the constraints you mention—but the distribution of productive capacity and the selling of the goods produced within any given country is likely to be greater, that is, the flourishing of trade as a whole is likely to be greater if you can, in effect, through the fixed exchange rates at least make a first approximation toward establishing all the world as your market.

And that will mean that there will be times when, in order to adapt successfully in a lasting way to the needs of making your own way in the other markets, you have to make some changes at home, perhaps more changes than would be necessary if you were isolated and had a defensive wall of a flexible exchange rate around your island.

But what I have tried to argue is that there will often be value in making the adjustment in the home economy that increases the capability to perform as a part of the world economy. With the use of an ample supply of reserves to tide over the period that the adjustments are occurring, it becomes possible to make these adjustments simply by changing the rate of increase in the domestic economy. Such adjustments never have to imply enforced unemployment, but they do require time. The end result, of that kind of environment, as I see it, is a wider area for the opportunities of freer trade.

Now, there are a good many other obstacles. Trying to mesh the trade with the capital movements becomes terribly complicated. But the objective that would be set by a fixed-rate system is that each country removes as it can, piece by piece, the other restrictions. Then it can enjoy the approximation that all are reaching for, in a sense, that is, a free trade area where differences among currencies do not matter.

THIRD SESSION

PROFESSOR JOSEPH ASCHEIM, George Washington University: I wonder what both speakers would think of the idea of conducting an experiment with respect to exchange rates for a duration to be specified by both of them as an appropriate one to disclose significant results of this experiment?

PROFESSOR FRIEDMAN: I don't really know how to answer that. I am willing to take any period of time that Dr. Roosa will give me.

DR. ROOSA: My answer is that I would just put it on a computer and run it through. That's the only one I'd be willing to take.

HOWARD PIQUET, Library of Congress: I would like to ask both gentlemen to comment on the band proposal, the proposal for widening the bands on foreign exchange rates as discussed primarily by Professor George N. Halm. I address the question to both gentlemen with a thought that maybe this is a compromise between the two positions.

PROFESSOR FRIEDMAN: My position is simple. I prefer a wide band to a narrow band and a wider band yet to a wide band. So that's a movement in the correct direction, although I am concerned that if you institute it, there is a possible tendency to drift up to one side of the band and then stick there.

DR. ROOSA: I haven't any hard and fast view about some widening of the band. I have thought that we ought to do some experimenting in that direction. So that would be part of the answer to your question, [Professor Ascheim]. We have begun experimentation with the few forward markets that exist by having the forward rates get to a range well outside the band of spot-rate fluctuation. As I recall, fluctuation has been by an amount at the most equal to about 4 percent per annum, in one case.

This is an elastic kind of relationship because as soon as the spot rate is pulled down toward the lower limit there has to be greater official support for the spot. Then the forward rate can't go any further. But this is the kind of experiment that I think deserves further testing, even though I am not conceding the principles of flexible rates. This is like deciding how much room to allow for expansion and contraction in a basically rigid steel structure. You want to discover how much you can safely allow to avoid the risk of cracking, while still keeping the structure itself fixed.

Incidentally, I quite agree with Milton that if the band were made very wide, the risk would be that rates would move to one end or the other and there still would not be room for variation. What you do have in such circumstances is a clear signal that there should have been a change in the parity. I think there may at some time be a place for a wider band. But this would be mainly as a means of getting a clearer indication of the time when a change in the fixed rate should be made.

HERBERT STEIN, Committee for Economic Development: Following up on that comment, under a fixed-rate system would controls over capital movements, exchange equalization tax, et cetera, be indications that lead to a change in the rate?

DR. ROOSA: No, the problem that these present restraints symbolize is the one that I have been hammering at here so hard ad nauseum tonight, that it is extremely difficult to get an equilibrium rate that takes into account at the same time both the major forces at work affecting capital movements and those affecting goods in trade.

It's particularly difficult because I suppose I was a little too easy in granting too much too quickly to Milton in this last exchange with respect even to the trade adjustment. This is because, alongside the influences of large and sustained capital movements, there are actually inelasticities in either supply or demand for the trade flows that are presumed to parallel the capital movements. And these inelasticities make it impossible to get the quick related adjustments in real terms, even if everything else were done properly.

So that there will often be times, in a world of substantial capital movement (and there will be more and more capital flows as we become more multilateralized, I hope) when divergence appears between the kind of equilibrium that is indicated by the pattern of capital flow over a given brief period—brief meaning two, three, four years—and the pattern that would prevail in purely trade terms.

I think we do have to live with some impediments of this kind. Now, Milton's answer is that a free rate has a radar eye and can pick out which of the things to adjust for and which not to adjust for. My feeling is that nobody can do that. Under any system we are going to have to have some selective arrangements when the imbalances, particularly of this kind between trade and capital flows, are not readily realizable, or readily reconcilable in a single rate.

PROFESSOR FRIEDMAN: But it is precisely, of course, the fact that it takes time to make the adjustments, that supply and demand are not perfectly elastic, which is why you want to have a flexible rate rather than a fixed rate. Let us suppose that there is a movement of capital that tends to come into a country and the country cannot adjust its production and consumption pattern instantaneously. To begin with, the rate will take on most of the burden. Then, as the adjustment is made, the rate will come back to that long-term rate which is appropriate to a full adjustment.

The great virtue of a market is precisely that short-term movements in prices can fill in the gap between the prior position and the new long-run position. The notion that somehow or other the people administering capital controls or voluntary exchange-rate restraints are going to be able to do their job in any kind of a delicate way is not a notion that you would find it very easy to support.

This is sort of off the track a little, but in your last interchange I realized all of a sudden that earlier I didn't give the right example in my remark about what your comments reminded me of. I suddenly realized that I was reminded of 1951 and the bond support pegging program.

Before the Federal Reserve gave up the pegging of the bond price, we heard all over the lot that a free market in bonds was going to be chaotic, that the interest rate might go heaven-high or down, there might be capital losses, savings institutions might well be wiped out by their capital losses, and that we needed some basic peg price on which the market could form its anticipation.

We abandoned the pegged price. None of these things happened in the bond market. And it seems to me you are doing the same thing over again. In each case—

DR. ROOSA: And, of course, the bond market has been surprisingly stable without government intervention ever since!

PROFESSOR FRIEDMAN: Well, you have had a good deal of Federal Reserve purchases and sales in the bond market for monetary purposes. That has made the bond market somewhat more unstable than it otherwise would have been without the government intervention. I'm glad to agree with you on that.

DR. ROOSA: You see, I didn't say it.

PROFESSOR FRIEDMAN: No, I know, but the implication is there.

PROFESSOR GOTTFRIED HABERLER, Harvard University: I should like to ask Dr. Roosa and Professor Friedman a question.

My question for Dr. Roosa is this: Are you not worried by the fact that we are getting into more and more controls of international payments, especially controls over capital movements? Only a few years ago you yourself used pretty strong language rejecting controls of capital flows.

[Professor Haberler later supplied a paragraph from a speech by Dr. Roosa in 1962 before the American Bankers Association to support his recollection:

This country rejects direct controls on the flow of capital not only because they would be inconsistent with our traditional and fundamental objectives of freeing trade and payments between countries, but for immediate dollars-and-cents reason—they would cost us more than they could possibly save. Our own money and capital markets are the most highly organized, most efficiently diversified, of any in the world. To try to impose controls over outward capital movements in any one sector of these markets—say bank loans— would only invite capital flight through many others, and to try instead a comprehensive approach—clamping the cold hand of capital issues controls, or credit rationing, over the entire sweep of the markets—would literally congeal the blood-stream of American capitalism.]

Your prediction that controls of one segment of the international capital market would "invite capital flight through other channels, has been proved correct by later events. The controls had to be extended to more and more areas.

How do you feel about that today? Don't you think the maintenance of fixed exchanges in the face of a continuing deficit has something to do with these disturbing developments?

DR. ROOSA: I am worried about a drift toward more controls, and just to show you how foolhardy I am, I am republishing several essays in which I have said that—in a book that will be out in another few months. So that I don't shrink from the embarrassment or from the implication.

I think what has happened has been the result of the interaction both of events from outside, which have been greater in impact than could have been visualized, and, let's face it, a comparative failure in the execution of domestic economic policy over the past year or year and a half.

To say that there have been these human failures is not to say that the objectives should not remain the same and that the system isn't going to, all things washing out, still be superior, because the same human beings are going to be at work, whether Milton likes it or not, manipulating the exchange rates of individual countries· under a system in which the superficial conditions of freedom or flexibility were accepted.

I grant that this is a regrettable trend, that it should be reversed, that we have not yet accomplished the reversal and though I don't want to drag in a real red herring, of course, there is something in the fact that we are fighting a war and we don't have any other form of exchange control or internal restraint.

I don't want to lean on that unfairly hard, but it does have something to do with the continuation of this whole array of unfortunate impediments to fully free capital movements now.

I would just say that as of the year 1964 the results of the other aspects of the domestic program, which had been undertaken beginning in 1961, were good enough that they produced a current account surplus of nearly $8 billion. That should have been enough to get away from the interest equalization tax and to make unnecessary the voluntary restraints program, but it wasn't.

PROFESSOR HABERLER: I cannot resist asking Dr. Roosa a second question. You speak of "manipulation" of the exchange rate under the system of flexible exchange rates. You said earlier that there would be a danger of "competitive devaluation."

Would such policies not be the very opposite of the

freely floating-rate system? In other words, you are not denying that the system may work, you are saying that countries will not be prepared to let the system of freely floating exchange rates operate.

DR. ROOSA: My argument is on two levels and I just argue that both are important. On the first level, as a matter of principle, I don't accept what 90 percent, at least, of the academic community in this country apparently accepts, that the theoretical case for fluctuating rates is a good case. I don't accept it.

But, going beyond that, I say, even if the case were good, even if I were going to grant you that this is the way in which a free-rate system should function, I go on to say that as a matter of hard fact individual monetary authorities, country by country, are not going to stand by and take the impact any more than they will take the impact of a deflationary policy that would provide more effective and quicker correction in the American economy.

They are going instead to temporize and find ways of accomplishing this result, as I think they should, more slowly, gradually, less precipitately. This pattern of adjustment to new norms in the internal economy is something, I think, that has to be taken as given, just as I think it must be taken as given that no nation is going to stand by and let its own exchange rate, in fact, be moved by other countries.

PROFESSOR FRIEDMAN: But you say take the impact. What impact? There isn't any impact. The floating exchange rate prevents the impact of those things that the country should not adapt to. You implicitly assume each time that all of the factors affecting exchange rates somehow or other hurt the individual country or require some real adjustment in the individual country. If what the exchange rate does is to make it unnecessary for them to adjust their own economy to external monetary changes, then what impact?

DR. ROOSA: This gets back to my monotonous point that you can't have it both ways. If all that happens is that the rate adjusts to keep the status quo, that's one thing. If, on the other hand, a rate change means that there is a change in the allocation of resources in both countries on both sides, then there are internal consequences.

PROFESSOR FRIEDMAN: Right, right.

DR. ROOSA: And if these internal consequences are to be allowed to work their way through, they will, from time to time, intrude upon the objectives currently being maintained for general economic policy. They will cause unemployment in some areas and an increase in employment somewhere else because the elasticities aren't perfect. You won't get the labor moving. You will get strain where the new demand is. You will get slack where there isn't demand.

You will then have domestic economic policy trying to cushion the impact and, before you know it, what you thought was being screened off by the change in rate has in fact been conditioned, altered, and given a new dimension by the fact that government, because of its other responsibilities, has moved in. And in the same way, before this even happens, the central bank, recognizing what is coming with an exchange-rate change, sees that in order to moderate the other kinds of policy action it may be impelled to take internally later, it should first move on the exchange rate.

This is exactly what happened in Canada during the period of 1950 to 1962. I was in Canada. I worked across the exchanges with the Canadian authorities. I sat at the trading desk with the officials of the Bank of Canada. I know how they at times had to jiggle the interest rate in order to maintain an appearance of relative stability in the Canadian dollar-U.S. dollar rate.

And this is supposed to be the example of what a flexible rate system can do. They had the ideal conditions: Nobody else in the world moving against them. One country able to move the rate against the whole world to its own advantage and they did it.

PROFESSOR FRIEDMAN: They hardly did it to their own advantage.

DR. ROOSA: In the end, of course, what they had to do was to recognize that the combination of structural relations between them and us, and occasional human failure in the execution of this set of maneuvers—human failures that correspond to the kind you are criticizing us for under the present system—the combination of these two things led them to see that the only workable arrangement was one under which they accepted some norms and went to work under them and set a parity.

PROFESSOR FRIEDMAN: I find it hard to accept the view that what happened had to happen and you don't really want to argue that either. You don't want to argue that every measure any country ever took was necessary—

DR. ROOSA: No, I just wanted to learn from that experience.

PROFESSOR FRIEDMAN: I do too. But let's go back for a moment. The existence of floating rates does not guarantee good internal policy in any country. It only permits it. It only facilitates it. So a country can have floating rates and bad internal policy. Canada did.

Second, I am not trying to have it both ways. What happens, each time you say that, is that you grant in principle that there may be two kinds of adjustments. Then you assume that there is only one kind and that somehow—

DR. ROOSA: There's only one rate.

PROFESSOR FRIEDMAN: You assume that there are no adjustments of rates that offset unnecessary adjustments. You assume that all adjustments of rates require physical adjustments because implicitly what you do is to assume that rates change only because of real changes in conditions of international trade.

Now, insofar as they do, under a fixed rate you have to make exactly the same kinds of adjustments to exactly those same kinds of changes and you have to do it in a way which will generate more difficult internal problems than under a flexible rate. Because, if there are changes in real forces of demand and supply, then to adjust to them with a fixed rate, you have to move your whole price level up and down.

Over and over again you implicitly assume that there is an adjustment mechanism under fixed rates which simply is not there. You state over and over again that all you need to have is a differential pace of adjustment and then you grant that we haven't had it. We've had exchange control and we've had one thing and another.

So I am not trying to have it both ways. What I am trying to say is that precisely because countries have committed themselves to internal policies of full employment, the amount of adjustment they are willing to undertake is limited. Let's not waste that. Let's reserve that adjustment capacity for those real changes in international trade which require adjustment capacity. Let's not fritter it away on forcing prices up and down, on introducing exchange controls or capital controls, because there have been monetary changes externally.

Finally, the argument for free rates is not that a country can't make a mistake, but that with free rates you have a chain in which, if one link is weak, the other links are not affected. If one country makes a mistake and goes off haywire, it pays the price, it pays it rather quickly, and it doesn't force unnecessary adjustments on other countries.

A fixed-rate system has the characteristic that, so long as it is maintained, a country which acts to disturb the system can, for a considerable time, be free of the necessity of paying for its actions.

DR. ROOSA: Milton, I can take everything critical that you said and say that the description applies in reverse, that this is exactly what happens with my definition of a flexible-rate system, which I insist must be one in which you can't assume that the central banks are nonparticipants.

PROFESSOR FRIEDMAN: Let me ask you a different question, a wholly different question, if I may. What kind of evidence would it require to persuade you that the fixed-rate system is not a viable one? What would have to happen in the world? How far would exchange rates have to get out of line? How much exchange control do you have to have? Can you conceive of a sequence of events over the next ten years so that ten years from now you would be willing to say, okay, a fixed-rate system is not going to work?

DR. ROOSA: Well, it's a pleasant invitation. I invite you to make the contrary suggestion—what do you think would make a fixed-rate system work, if it's not working already? But I simply cannot see how a flexible-rate system could work. I just am unable to give you that much satisfaction, much as I would like to try.

PROFESSOR FRIEDMAN: I'm not asking you to say how it can work. I am pursuing the line that Professor Haberler raised. Professor Haberler said to you, you believe in free trade and so do I. You believe in free capital movements. You and I alike agree—

DR. ROOSA: Yes.

PROFESSOR FRIEDMAN: —that the development of exchange controls and so on is congealing the blood of capitalism. All right, now, following up on Professor Haberler's question, how far does the blood have to congeal before you will be willing to say there is something wrong with the system?

DR. ROOSA: I put it the other way around. If the blood congeals, the same conditions of national commitment to national objectives that I have been talking about as relevant here will lead not to a flexible-rate system but to a system of organized trading blocs in which the conditions of a fixed-rate system can be preserved within a smaller geographical area.

Now, I think this would certainly be unfortunate for the pattern of evolution in world trade and of economic and political relations. But I cannot conceive of any congealing that would reach a stage where the world and the people that I know in it are going to turn, in fact, to a flexible system because the effects of a flexible system are clear enough. They are going to want to preserve, within whatever area they can make coherent, the advantages of the fixed-rate system within that area.

PROFESSOR FRIEDMAN: But then you are really evading the issue, Bob.

DR. ROOSA: No, I am just giving you the only alternative.

PROFESSOR FRIEDMAN: No, you're not, because whether they turn to the flexible-rate system or not depends on whether people like you are willing to look at it clearly and willing to face up to the issues of a flexible-rate system and answer each case not by the statement, "We won't have it," but rather ask yourself the question, "How would it in fact operate?" Whether they turn toward a flexible rate or toward the narrow regional blocs will depend in large part on what people like you urge and recommend them to do.

And to say I am not even going to look and examine and study in detail how a flexible-rate system will work because no country will adopt it—

DR. ROOSA: All I am trying to say is that, having at least looked at a flexible rate long enough to engage in this little debate, the look that I have taken convinces me that it is not either theoretically sound or operationally practicable and therefore I ask myself, What does happen if the present system breaks down and it can't be continued? What is the alternative?

PROFESSOR FRIEDMAN: What do you mean by the statement it is not theoretically sound? That seems to use the word "theory" in a different sense than I understand it.

DR. ROOSA: Conceptually.

PROFESSOR FRIEDMAN: I don't understand what you mean. I have read your paper. There is not a word in there which can be interpreted as saying that a system of floating exchange rates is not conceptually sound.

DR. ROOSA: There are really two principal points on which it hinges and then I suppose a number of other ancillary ones. The first is this point that we have labored pretty hard, the assumption that adjustment will occur instantaneously, that countries can accept it as an instantaneous adjustment and that there is an elasticity on both sides which permits this to occur without strain.

PROFESSOR FRIEDMAN: But those are not valid points of a floating-rate system. The second of them is a political judgment. So let's leave it out for a moment.

DR. ROOSA: All right.

PROFESSOR FRIEDMAN: We want to know whether it's theoretically sound. Do you deny that the market will set a price?

DR. ROOSA: I deny that an actual market will exist.

PROFESSOR FRIEDMAN: You deny that a market will exist in exchange?

DR. ROOSA: I do, yes.

PROFESSOR FRIEDMAN: In foreign exchanges?

DR. ROOSA: You will find, if all countries have no fixed parity, that instead, because there isn't a real going and lasting market, the relationships that will begin to develop will be the kinds which will lead to the creation of the bloc system that I have described; fixed rates within each bloc, and barter among them.

PROFESSOR FRIEDMAN: You don't believe that there is a securities market in the world? You don't believe that there is an international stock market and you don't believe there are bond markets and you don't believe there are markets for commodities?

DR. ROOSA: Indeed I do. My partners and I trade

in most of them every day—at fixed rates of exchange. But the difference between all of these things and money is that the money which has to represent the composite of all these things, the numeraire in which they all have to be measured, has to have some capability of stability. That is the capability which you also want. Without it, the drive of every organized society is going to be to find that stability.

PROFESSOR HABERLER: My question, addressed to Professor Friedman, is this: I was surprised when you said at the beginning of your speech that you would be in favor of fixed exchange rates, if we have a real gold standard. By that you meant, I believe, that the quantity of money was fixed for the whole world.

PROFESSOR FRIEDMAN: No. What I meant was a unified currency system among the nations of the world in which there was a single money, gold, which had different names in different countries. It might be called the dollar in the United States. But a dollar was defined as one thirty-fifth of an ounce of gold and a pound was defined as so much, so that you had in the world as a whole the equivalent of what we have among the different states in this country.

PROFESSOR HABERLER: Does that not mean that the quantity of money, in terms of gold, is fixed for the whole world?

PROFESSOR FRIEDMAN: Oh, yes, indeed. I misunderstood you. I thought you meant by fixed that it is constant.

PROFESSOR HABERLER: Then let me ask this question: Suppose under such a monetary arrangement one part of the world expands faster than the other. Would that not mean that the fast expanding area would drain money away from the slowly expanding area and would inflict a painful deflation on the latter? Would it not be preferable to have flexible rates?

PROFESSOR FRIEDMAN: Yes, it would.

PROFESSOR HABERLER: So, in that case you would probably again drop the fixed rate.

PROFESSOR FRIEDMAN: As a purely technical matter, there is no doubt that floating exchange rates would be preferable but I do believe that the political argument for a unified currency is a valid argument. If you have a real gold standard, I would argue that the adjustment would be so gradual and slow that you would not in fact have a major real problem of the kind that you are suggesting.

PROFESSOR HABERLER: This is a factual assumption which does not happen. Half of the world expands at a very fast rate and the other half does not.

PROFESSOR FRIEDMAN: You see, my view, in contrast to Bob's is that what central banks do in practice is not solely to smooth out minor movements. They do that sometimes but what they often do is to prevent adjustments which would be minor and which instead accumulate into major problems. Even if nine times out of ten when they smooth out a minor movement they prevent an unnecessary adjustment, the one time they make a mistake, they convert what otherwise would have been a minor problem of adjustment into a sizable problem.

My hunch is that under a real gold standard, because adjustments would be set in train very gradually, because a slight discrepancy between two countries would produce a slight adjustment, the problem would be what it now is among the different areas of the United States, where major discrepancies do not accumulate. Maybe I am wrong on that but that was the assumption under which I was operating.

JAROSLAV HABR, Academy of Sciences, Prague, Czechoslovakia: I have listened to both discussions, both lectures, and I would like to express my thanks for this unique opportunity for someone who is coming from Central Europe. But, in one sense, it was not a unique experience. It seemed to me sometimes that I was listening to our top, top planner and our top, top reformer. And you know who is who.

It is relatively easy to make a conceptual framework either for the present existing world or for some future world, but it is always very difficult to create a conceptual framework for a transitional period. It appears to me to be difficult for someone who believes in the present world not to be rather skeptical about the new constructions of the future. And on the other side, those who are making the constructions are perhaps underrating the programs of the representatives of the present world.

DR. ROOSA: We do know each who we are.

PROFESSOR FRIEDMAN: I will get even with him later for calling me a reformer.

PROFESSOR FRANK TAMAGNA, American University: I have been listening to you with some surprise, because one of the things you are saying is that once the adjustments have been made, either of the systems would work.

PROFESSOR FRIEDMAN: I think the basic difference, Professor Tamagna, is whether, if countries do not follow the right policy, the burden then falls on the country which has made a mistake or it is spread throughout the system and so disturbs the whole system.

In my opinion, the great virtue of a world in which exchange rates are free to vary but in which countries are able to follow stable policies so the rates are in fact relatively stable, is that a country which departs from the rules itself pays the price and, therefore, the chain is as strong as its strongest link.

The defect of the fixed exchange-rate system on the level that you are raising is that if a country does not follow what we regard as the correct policy it can, for a considerable time, shift the burden onto the other countries. This produces difficulties in the whole system so that the chain is only as strong as its weakest link.

DR. ROOSA: On the same point, we have just reached the stage where I think Milton has made his most telling thrust at the system I am defending. I recognize that the greatest defect, and I didn't have the temerity to advertise it on my own, is the asymmetry of this impact on deficit and surplus countries. Surplus countries can, if they are so inclined, get off easy and shift most of the burden of correction onto the deficit countries.

I think this is part of a fundamental defect which does require considerable additional effort both to devise norms of behavior and to impose them through agreed means. I grant that this is the area in which the most needs to be done and where the present system is, in fact, weakest.

On the other side, I do not feel that you can say that a choice between the systems becomes a matter of indifference. It is important to see that the pattern of reactions that is created, once the system is in being, the pattern of reactions that is created on the part of the private sector that engages in the trade and provides the investment, will be that which has the greatest assurance of maximizing the growth and the rational distribution of resources around the world.

Now, if it were true that Milton's system would always produce stable rates, then I think we would have something close to the equivalent of a single currency in the world and we would get the distribution of resources that is ideal. My difference hinges at least in part but importantly on the fact that I do not believe that the conditions of a flexible-rate system will make it possible for the ordinary merchant and trader and banker and investor to have the conditions of reasonable assurance, the benchmarks for making choices, the reasonable stability of conditions for committing resources, that is necessary to get the greatest result.

With all its imperfections, and granting that, as I say, I think Milton has put his finger on what is a major defect of a fixed-rate system, I still feel that in the total result the gain, because of its influence on the private commercial sector, is greater and will continue to be greater under a fixed-rate system. I do think that the flourishing of trade and capital flows that we have seen, with all of the troubles, in the last decade since convertibility was restored, provides some evidence to support my argument.

PROFESSOR FRIEDMAN: But those conditions, Bob, under which floating rates will not be stable, are precisely the conditions under which your fixed rates can be maintained only by exchange controls, interferences with trade, and so on. And these have the same disruptive effects, I would say much worse ones, because at least if floating rates aren't stable the countries that go off half-cocked are the ones that bear the burden.

DR. ROOSA: Not always. But partly my opposition comes also because I think the mere existence of the flexible system creates an environment, as I say, for destabilizing speculation at times. But on that we really can't agree. We just identify our differences.

PROFESSOR FRIEDMAN: I should say that I once wrote an essay entitled "In Defense of Destabilizing Speculation," because I am willing to go so far as to say that in point of fact if there is destabilizing speculation there is nothing wrong with that either. That simply means that the speculators are making a gift to the countries involved. If there is destabilizing speculation, speculators lose. Who gains? Essentially the citizens of the two countries who provide gambling services to the speculators.

DR. ROOSA: On that difference I am afraid we will have to rest. As I said in the beginning, I will leave with even more respect, if that's possible, for your capability of making any case plausible and persuasive and I will undertake to study a little further the offer that you have given me to find the conditions under which a flexible system could possibly be considered. There has to be a presumption, I confess, that such a brilliant jockey could not have chosen a horse as poor as the one I think I see.

FOOTNOTES

SECOND LECTURE
Page 66

[1] My own appraisal of the issues to be resolved in providing an acceptable supplement to gold through multi-national creation of a new reserve asset will appear in *The Dollar and World Liquidity*, scheduled for publication by Random House in September, 1967.

DISCUSSION

SECOND SESSION
Page 161

[1] Including time deposits the rise was about 10 percent, but not all time deposits can be considered a part of the active money supply.

	DATE DUE	